RAISING GOOD HUMANS

A GUIDE TO CHARACTER DEVELOPMENT

DR. MINAKSHI BANSAL

Copyright © Dr. Minakshi Bansal
All Rights Reserved.

This book has been self-published with all reasonable efforts taken to make the material error-free by the author. No part of this book shall be used, reproduced in any manner whatsoever without written permission from the author, except in the case of brief quotations embodied in critical articles and reviews.

The Author of this book is solely responsible and liable for its content including but not limited to the views, representations, descriptions, statements, information, opinions and references ["Content"]. The Content of this book shall not constitute or be construed or deemed to reflect the opinion or expression of the Publisher or Editor. Neither the Publisher nor Editor endorse or approve the Content of this book or guarantee the reliability, accuracy or completeness of the Content published herein and do not make any representations or warranties of any kind, express or implied, including but not limited to the implied warranties of merchantability, fitness for a particular purpose. The Publisher and Editor shall not be liable whatsoever for any errors, omissions, whether such errors or omissions result from negligence, accident, or any other cause or claims for loss or damages of any kind, including without limitation, indirect or consequential loss or damage arising out of use, inability to use, or about the reliability, accuracy or sufficiency of the information contained in this book.

Made with ❤ on the Notion Press Platform
www.notionpress.com

DEDICATION

To those who dare to chase their dreams against the odds, who find strength in adversity, and who never falter in their pursuit of greatness. This work is dedicated to the believers, the dreamers, and the relentless seekers of light in the darkest of nights.

♡♡♡

Contents

Contents

Contents

Prayer

"Om Bhadram Karnebhih Shrinuyama Devah

Bhadram Pashyemakshabhiryajatrah

Sthirairangais Tushtuvamsastanubhih

Vyashema Devahitam Yadayuh

Svasti Na Indro Vriddhashravah

Svasti Nah Pusha Vishwavedah

Svasti Nastarkshyo Arishtanemih

Svasti No Brihaspatir Dadhatu

Om Shantih Shantih Shantih"

This mantra is a prayer for universal well-being, invoking the blessings of various deities for protection, health, and happiness. It emphasizes the importance of experiencing the auspicious through all senses and living a life aligned with divine purpose. The repetition of "Shantih" at the end signifies a deep desire for peace in the individual, the environment, and the universe at large. This mantra is often recited as a prayer for peace, prosperity, and the physical and spiritual well-being of all beings.

▷▷▷

About The Author

This book represents the culmination of extensive research and meticulous analysis, incorporating a diverse range of sources, including numerous books, scholarly studies, and personal experiences. Additionally, I have scoured various websites to gather relevant information and data essential for the compilation of this work. I have taken every precaution to ensure the accuracy of the information presented and have diligently cited all sources to acknowledge their contributions.

From her earliest days, Minakshi was distinguished by an insatiable appetite for reading. Her literary universe was inhabited by characters and narratives that spanned ethical tales, motivational and inspirational stories, and the mythic parables imbued with life lessons. This voracious reading habit was not merely for personal edification but was driven by a desire to distill and disseminate the essence of these narratives to foster the development of students and peers alike. She was particularly captivated by the lives and teachings of historical figures and spiritual leaders such as Adi Shankaracharya, Swami Vivekananda, Dr. APJ Abdul Kalam, Mahamana Pandit Madan Mohan Malviya, Mahatma Gandhi, Sardar Vallabhai Patel, and Vinoba Bhave, among others. Their philosophies and life stories fueled her ambition to embody their ideals of resilience, selflessness, and relentless pursuit of knowledge.

Dr. Minakshi's academic and practical engagement with psychology has been equally noteworthy. As a research scholar, her focus has been on exploring the intricate tapestry of the human psyche, aiming to unlock the potential for psychological well-being and societal harmony. Her scholarly work is complemented by her active involvement in social work, where she employs her academic insights to make tangible differences in the lives of the underprivileged. Her endeavours in social work are characterized by an innovative approach that combines traditional wisdom with contemporary psychological practices to address the multifaceted challenges faced by these communities.

Her artistic talents, another facet of her diverse capabilities, are not merely a personal passion but also serve as a medium through which she communicates and connects with others. Her art, rich in symbolism and emotional depth, reflects her philosophical inquiries and social concerns, offering viewers a glimpse into the breadth of her intellect and the depth of her compassion.

In addition to her contributions to the arts and social sciences, Dr. Minakshi has embraced the healing arts of Pranic Healing, mastering the techniques developed by Master Choa Kok Sui. This practice, which focuses on the manipulation of Prana or life energy to heal the body and aura, has been both a personal journey of discovery and a means through which she extends her healing touch to others. Her proficiency in Pranic Healing is complemented by her advocacy and teaching of various forms of meditation aimed at rejuvenation, personal betterment, and the cultivation of harmony within individuals and communities alike.

Dr. Minakshi's life is a narrative of relentless pursuit, not just of personal achievement but of the upliftment and empowerment of society at large. Her diverse interests and talents—spanning the arts, literature, psychology, and the healing practices—converge on a singular path of service. She embodies the spirit of the luminaries who inspired her, channelling their legacy through her actions and teachings. Through her books, art, and social initiatives, she continues to inspire a new generation to embark on their own journeys of self-discovery, resilience, and altruism.

Her commitment to social betterment, particularly her focus on uplifting underprivileged children, reflects a deep understanding of the transformative potential of education and personal development. By integrating her knowledge of psychology, her artistic sensibilities, and her healing practices, Dr. Bansal has developed a holistic approach to social work that addresses both the immediate needs and the long-term well-being of the communities she serves.

As an author, Dr. Minakshi's writings offer a blend of inspirational insights, practical wisdom, and reflective contemplations drawn from her extensive reading and life experiences. Her books serve as a guide for those seeking to navigate the complexities of life with grace, resilience, and purpose. Through her narratives, she extends an invitation to her readers to explore the depths of their own potential and to contribute meaningfully to the collective well-being of society.

In Dr. Minakshi Bansal, we find a remarkable synthesis of the artist, the scholar, the healer, and the social activist. Her life's work stands as a beacon of hope and a source of inspiration for individuals seeking to make a difference in the world. Her story is a compelling reminder of the power of individual action, rooted in compassion and driven by a profound commitment to the betterment of humanity. Dr. Minakshi's legacy is not just in the tangible outcomes of her efforts but in the enduring spirit of inquiry, empathy, and service that she embodies.

ᐅᐅᐅ

Preface

Writing this book has been a journey of exploration and reflection, born out of a deep desire to understand and nurture the qualities that define good human beings. As a mother, educator, and observer of the world, I have often pondered the essential elements that contribute to a child's character development. In an age where external influences are pervasive and often overwhelming, it has become more crucial than ever to focus on the core values that form the bedrock of a strong, compassionate, and resilient character.

This book is a culmination of years of personal experiences, research, and insights gathered from various facets of my life. The motivation to write it stemmed from my own observations and the myriad conversations I have had with other parents, educators, and caregivers who share the same concerns and aspirations. We all strive to raise children who are not only successful in the conventional sense but also kind, empathetic, responsible, and capable of navigating life's complexities with grace and integrity.

One of the foundational aspects of character development that I explore is empathy. Empathy is the ability to understand and share the feelings of others, a skill that is essential for forming meaningful connections and fostering a compassionate society. From a young age, children can learn to recognize and respond to the emotions of those around them. Through simple acts of kindness, active listening, and role-playing, we can teach our children to step into others' shoes and appreciate their perspectives. Modeling empathetic behavior ourselves is perhaps the most powerful tool we have, as children often emulate the actions and attitudes of the adults they look up to.

Respect is another cornerstone of good character, encompassing both self-respect and respect for others. Teaching children to value themselves and those around them involves setting clear expectations, providing consistent discipline, and fostering an environment where respectful behavior is the norm. It is through everyday interactions that children learn the importance of treating others with kindness and consideration, whether it's sharing their toys, listening attentively, or expressing gratitude. By consistently reinforcing these behaviors and recognizing their efforts, we help our children internalize the value of respect.

Honesty, a principle that builds trust and integrity, is crucial for developing a strong moral character. Encouraging honesty in children involves creating a safe space where they feel comfortable telling the truth, even when it's difficult. It's important to approach dishonesty with understanding and guidance rather than punishment, helping children understand the impact of their actions and the importance of living authentically. When children see honesty modeled in the behaviors of their parents and caregivers, they are more likely to embrace this value themselves.

Kindness is a simple yet profound quality that can transform lives and communities. Teaching children to be kind involves encouraging them to think about the needs and feelings of others and to act in ways that bring joy and comfort. Acts of kindness, no matter how small, can have a ripple effect, creating a culture of generosity and compassion. Whether it's helping a friend, sharing their possessions, or simply offering a smile, these acts of kindness reinforce the importance of caring for one another.

Responsibility is about taking ownership of one's actions and understanding the consequences. Teaching children to be responsible involves giving them age-appropriate tasks and allowing them to experience the natural outcomes of their choices. By holding them accountable and guiding them through their mistakes, we prepare them to be conscientious and dependable individuals. Responsibility also involves teaching children to manage their time and resources effectively, skills that will serve them well throughout their lives.

Courage is the ability to face challenges and adversity with strength and determination. Encouraging courage in children involves creating a supportive environment where they feel safe to take risks and try new things. Celebrating their efforts and perseverance, rather than just their successes, helps build resilience and bravery. It is important to teach children that failure is a natural part of the learning process and that each setback is an opportunity for growth and improvement.

Patience, the ability to wait calmly and without frustration, is an essential skill for navigating life's inevitable delays and setbacks. Teaching patience involves modeling calm behavior, setting realistic expectations, and providing opportunities for children to practice waiting. Engaging in activities that require delayed gratification, such as saving money for a desired toy or waiting their turn in a game, can help children develop this important skill.

Gratitude is the practice of recognizing and appreciating the positive aspects of life. Teaching gratitude involves encouraging children to express thanks for the people, experiences, and things they value. Practices such as keeping a gratitude journal and writing thank-you notes can help instill gratitude as a daily habit. Recognizing and celebrating the efforts of others and expressing appreciation for the good things in life can foster a positive and appreciative mindset.

Humility involves recognizing one's limitations and valuing the contributions of others. Teaching humility requires modeling modest behavior, encouraging children to acknowledge their mistakes, and helping them understand that everyone has unique strengths and weaknesses. Balancing self-esteem with humility ensures that children feel confident and capable while being respectful and appreciative of others.

Generosity is the willingness to give and share without expecting anything in return. Teaching generosity involves encouraging children to share their time, resources, and talents with others. Participating in charitable activities and discussing the importance of helping others can help foster a generous spirit. By highlighting the joy and satisfaction that comes from giving, we can help children develop a lifelong commitment to generosity.

Self-discipline is the ability to control one's impulses and behaviors. Teaching self-discipline requires setting clear expectations, providing consistent consequences, and encouraging children to practice self-control. Activities that require focus and perseverance, such as completing homework before playtime or saving money for a special purchase, can help children develop self-discipline.

Perseverance is the ability to keep going despite difficulties and setbacks. Teaching perseverance involves encouraging children to set goals, providing support and encouragement, and helping them learn from their mistakes. Celebrating efforts and progress helps build resilience and determination, teaching children that persistence and hard work can lead to success.

Optimism is the practice of focusing on the positive aspects of life and maintaining a hopeful outlook. Teaching optimism involves modeling positive behavior, encouraging children to reframe negative situations, and helping them focus on their strengths and successes. Engaging in activities that promote positive thinking can help nurture an optimistic mindset, which is essential for resilience and overall well-being.

Service is the act of helping others and contributing to the community. Teaching service involves providing opportunities for children to engage in acts of kindness and volunteerism. Discussing the impact of their actions and encouraging them to think about how they can make a difference helps instill a sense of responsibility and generosity. Service not only benefits those who receive help but also enriches the lives of those who give.

Fairness involves treating others equitably and justly. Teaching fairness requires modeling fair behavior, setting clear rules and expectations, and encouraging children to consider the perspectives of others. Engaging in discussions about fairness and providing opportunities to practice fair decision-making helps foster a sense of equality and integrity.

Forgiveness is the ability to let go of resentment and move forward after being wronged. Teaching forgiveness involves modeling forgiving behavior, encouraging children to express their feelings, and helping them understand the importance of letting go of grudges. Discussing the benefits of forgiveness and providing opportunities to practice it helps nurture a forgiving and compassionate spirit.

Cooperation involves working together towards a common goal. Teaching cooperation requires providing opportunities for children to engage in group activities, encouraging teamwork, and modeling cooperative behavior. Discussing the importance of collaboration and helping children understand the value of different perspectives helps foster a sense of unity and mutual respect.

Curiosity is the desire to learn and explore. Teaching curiosity involves encouraging children to ask questions, providing opportunities for exploration and discovery, and modeling a curious mindset. Engaging in activities that stimulate curiosity helps nurture a sense of wonder and intellectual growth.

Peacefulness involves maintaining calm and resolving conflicts harmoniously. Teaching peacefulness involves modeling calm behavior, providing opportunities to practice relaxation techniques, and encouraging children to resolve conflicts respectfully. Engaging in activities that promote mindfulness and emotional regulation helps nurture a sense of peace and tranquility.

As I reflect on the values and principles discussed in this book, I am reminded of the profound impact that these lessons have had on my own life and the lives of those around me. Each value contributes to the overall development of a child's character and ability to interact positively with the world. Through consistent modeling, positive reinforcement, and creating an environment that fosters growth and learning, we can help our children internalize these values and carry them into adulthood.

The journey of raising good humans is not without its challenges, but it is a journey worth taking. By investing in the moral and ethical development of our children, we are laying the foundation for a better future for all. As parents, caregivers, and educators, we have the privilege and responsibility to guide the next generation in becoming compassionate, resilient, and responsible individuals. It is my hope that this book serves as a valuable resource and inspiration for those who share this important mission.

In writing this book, I have drawn from my own experiences, the wisdom of others, and the timeless lessons of character development. It is a labor of love, born out of a deep commitment to nurturing the best in our children and ourselves. As you embark on your own journey of raising good humans, may you find encouragement, guidance, and hope within these pages. Together, we can create a world where kindness, integrity, and empathy are the guiding principles of our lives.

Dr. Minakshi Bansal
Social Activist
Ahmedabad, Gujarat, Bharat

❦❦❦

ONE

The Foundation of Character: Understanding the Basics of Moral Development

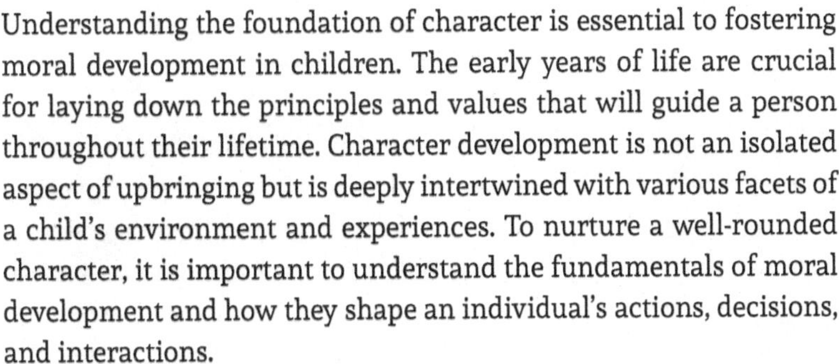

Understanding the foundation of character is essential to fostering moral development in children. The early years of life are crucial for laying down the principles and values that will guide a person throughout their lifetime. Character development is not an isolated aspect of upbringing but is deeply intertwined with various facets of a child's environment and experiences. To nurture a well-rounded character, it is important to understand the fundamentals of moral development and how they shape an individual's actions, decisions, and interactions.

Moral development begins at a young age, influenced by the child's family, culture, education, and social interactions. From infancy, children start to observe and absorb the behaviors, attitudes, and values of those around them. They are highly impressionable and learn through imitation and reinforcement. Parents and caregivers play a pivotal role in this process, serving as the primary models of behavior and morality.

One of the key aspects of moral development is the establishment of a secure and nurturing environment. When children feel safe, loved, and valued, they are more likely to develop positive traits such as empathy, kindness, and respect. A supportive environment fosters a sense of trust and belonging, which is fundamental for moral growth. In such an atmosphere, children learn that their actions have consequences and that their choices matter. This understanding is the cornerstone of developing a moral compass.

Empathy is a crucial component of moral development. It is the ability to understand and share the feelings of others. Empathy helps children connect with others on an emotional level, fostering compassion and kindness. To cultivate empathy, it is important for parents and caregivers to model empathetic behavior. This can be done by acknowledging and validating a child's emotions, encouraging them to express their feelings, and teaching them to consider the perspectives of others. Activities such as reading stories, discussing characters' emotions, and engaging in role-playing can also enhance a child's empathetic abilities.

Respect is another foundational element of character. It involves recognizing the inherent worth of oneself and others. Teaching children to respect themselves and those around them is essential for building healthy relationships and a harmonious society. Respect can be instilled by setting clear expectations for behavior, providing consistent discipline, and modeling respectful interactions. It is important to emphasize that respect is a two-way street; children should be treated with respect and, in turn, learn to treat others the same way.

Honesty is a virtue that lies at the heart of moral character. It involves being truthful and transparent in one's actions and words. Honesty builds trust and credibility, which are essential for meaningful relationships. To foster honesty in children, it is important to create an environment where they feel safe to tell the truth, even when it is difficult. Encouraging open communication, praising honesty, and addressing dishonesty calmly and constructively are effective ways to promote this virtue. Children should understand that honesty is not just about telling the truth but also about living authentically and with integrity.

Kindness is a trait that enhances the quality of life for both the giver and the receiver. Acts of kindness, whether big or small, contribute to a sense of community and well-being. Teaching children to be kind involves encouraging them to think about how their actions affect others and to engage in acts of generosity and compassion. Kindness can be nurtured by involving children in community service, practicing gratitude, and recognizing and celebrating kind behaviors.

Responsibility is a key aspect of moral development. It involves taking ownership of one's actions and understanding the impact they have on oneself and others. Teaching children responsibility requires giving them age-appropriate tasks and allowing them to experience the consequences of their actions. It is important to encourage independence while providing guidance and support. By holding children accountable and helping them learn from their mistakes, we prepare them to be responsible and conscientious individuals.

Courage is the ability to face challenges and adversity with strength and determination. It is an important trait that enables individuals to stand up for what is right, even in the face of fear or opposition.

To foster courage in children, it is important to create an environment where they feel supported and encouraged to take risks and try new things. Celebrating their efforts, rather than just their successes, and teaching them to view failure as a learning opportunity can help build resilience and bravery.

Patience is a virtue that helps individuals navigate the ups and downs of life with grace and composure. It involves the ability to wait calmly and without frustration. Teaching children patience requires modeling calm behavior, setting realistic expectations, and providing opportunities for them to practice waiting. Engaging in activities that require delayed gratification, such as gardening or cooking, can help children develop patience and understand the value of persistence.

Gratitude is the practice of recognizing and appreciating the positive aspects of life. It fosters a positive outlook and enhances well-being. Teaching children gratitude involves encouraging them to express thanks for the people, experiences, and things they value. Keeping a gratitude journal, writing thank-you notes, and regularly discussing the things they are grateful for can help instill this practice. Gratitude helps children develop a sense of contentment and appreciation for what they have, rather than constantly seeking more.

Humility is the quality of being modest and respectful. It involves recognizing one's limitations and valuing the contributions of others. Teaching children humility requires modeling modest behavior, encouraging them to acknowledge their mistakes, and helping them understand that everyone has unique strengths and weaknesses. It is important to balance self-esteem with humility, ensuring that children feel confident and capable while also being respectful and appreciative of others.

Generosity is the willingness to give and share without expecting anything in return. It enhances social connections and contributes to a sense of community. Teaching children generosity involves encouraging them to share their time, resources, and talents with others. Participating in charitable activities, such as donating toys or volunteering, and discussing the importance of helping others can help foster a generous spirit.

Self-discipline is the ability to control one's impulses and behaviors. It is essential for achieving long-term goals and maintaining healthy habits. Teaching children self-discipline requires setting clear expectations, providing consistent consequences, and encouraging them to practice self-control. Activities that require focus and perseverance, such as sports or music, can help children develop self-discipline.

Perseverance is the ability to keep going despite difficulties and setbacks. It is a crucial trait for achieving success and overcoming challenges. Teaching children perseverance involves encouraging them to set goals, providing support and encouragement, and helping them learn from their mistakes. Celebrating their efforts and progress, rather than just their achievements, can help build resilience and determination.

Optimism is the practice of focusing on the positive aspects of life and maintaining a hopeful outlook. It enhances well-being and helps individuals cope with challenges. Teaching children optimism involves modeling positive behavior, encouraging them to reframe negative situations, and helping them focus on their strengths and successes. Engaging in activities that promote positive thinking, such as keeping a gratitude journal or practicing mindfulness, can help nurture an optimistic mindset.

Service is the act of helping others and contributing to the community. It fosters a sense of purpose and connection. Teaching children the joy of service involves providing opportunities for them to engage in acts of kindness and volunteerism. Discussing the impact of their actions and encouraging them to think about how they can make a difference in the lives of others can help instill a sense of responsibility and generosity.

Fairness is the practice of treating others equitably and justly. It involves recognizing and respecting the rights and needs of others. Teaching children fairness requires modeling fair behavior, setting clear rules and expectations, and encouraging them to consider the perspectives of others. Engaging in discussions about fairness and justice, and providing opportunities for them to practice fair decision-making, can help foster a sense of equality and integrity.

Forgiveness is the ability to let go of resentment and move forward after being wronged. It is essential for maintaining healthy relationships and emotional well-being. Teaching children forgiveness involves modeling forgiving behavior, encouraging them to express their feelings, and helping them understand the importance of letting go of grudges. Discussing the benefits of forgiveness and providing opportunities for them to practice it can help nurture a forgiving and compassionate spirit.

Cooperation is the practice of working together towards a common goal. It enhances social connections and contributes to a sense of community. Teaching children cooperation involves providing opportunities for them to engage in group activities, encouraging teamwork, and modeling cooperative behavior. Discussing the importance of collaboration and helping them understand the value of different perspectives can help foster a sense of unity and mutual respect.

Curiosity is the desire to learn and explore. It fosters a love for learning and enhances cognitive development. Teaching children the power of curiosity involves encouraging them to ask questions, providing opportunities for exploration and discovery, and modeling a curious mindset. Engaging in activities that stimulate their curiosity, such as science experiments or nature walks, can help nurture their sense of wonder and intellectual growth.

Peacefulness is the practice of maintaining calm and resolving conflicts harmoniously. It enhances emotional well-being and contributes to a harmonious society. Teaching children peacefulness involves modeling calm behavior, providing opportunities for them to practice relaxation techniques, and encouraging them to resolve conflicts respectfully. Engaging in activities that promote mindfulness and emotional regulation, such as yoga or meditation, can help nurture a sense of peace and tranquility.

The foundation of character is built upon a complex interplay of various virtues and values. By understanding and nurturing these elements, we can guide children towards moral development and help them become well-rounded, compassionate, and responsible individuals. Character development is a lifelong journey, and it is our responsibility as parents, caregivers, and educators to provide the guidance and support needed for children to navigate this path successfully. Through consistent modeling, positive reinforcement, and creating an environment that fosters growth and learning, we can help raise good humans who contribute positively to society and lead fulfilling lives.

ppp

"In the symphony of life, every note counts, for it is the discord that births the most beautiful melodies."

♡♡♡

TWO

BUILDING EMPATHY: TEACHING CHILDREN TO CARE FOR OTHERS

Building empathy in children is a fundamental aspect of nurturing their emotional and social development. Empathy, the ability to understand and share the feelings of others, is essential for forming healthy relationships, fostering kindness, and creating a compassionate society. Teaching children to care for others involves a multifaceted approach that includes modeling empathetic behavior, providing opportunities for perspective-taking, and encouraging compassionate actions.

From an early age, children are naturally curious about the emotions and experiences of those around them. This curiosity provides a perfect foundation for cultivating empathy. Parents and caregivers play a crucial role in this process, as they are the primary models of empathetic behavior. By demonstrating empathy in everyday interactions, adults can show children how to recognize and respond to the emotions of others. Simple actions such as listening attentively, validating feelings, and offering comfort can have a profound impact on a child's understanding of empathy.

One of the most effective ways to teach empathy is through active listening. When children express their feelings, whether they are happy, sad, frustrated, or excited, it is important for adults to listen without judgment and show genuine interest. This validates the child's emotions and teaches them that their feelings are important and worthy of attention. By practicing active listening, adults can help children feel understood and supported, which in turn encourages them to extend the same level of understanding to others.

Another key aspect of building empathy is helping children develop the ability to take the perspective of others. Perspective-taking involves imagining oneself in another person's situation and understanding their thoughts, feelings, and motivations. This skill can be nurtured through various activities and discussions. Reading stories and discussing the characters' emotions and actions is a powerful way to engage children in perspective-taking. By asking questions such as "How do you think this character feels?" or "What would you do if you were in their situation?" adults can encourage children to think beyond their own experiences and consider the viewpoints of others.

Role-playing is another effective technique for teaching empathy. Through role-playing activities, children can practice putting themselves in different situations and exploring how they might feel and respond. This helps them develop a deeper understanding of the emotions and experiences of others. For example, role-playing scenarios such as comforting a friend who is upset or standing up for someone who is being bullied can help children practice empathetic responses in a safe and supportive environment.

Encouraging children to express their own emotions is also essential for building empathy. When children are comfortable talking about their feelings, they are better able to understand and relate to the emotions of others. Adults can create an open and accepting environment where children feel safe to share their thoughts and feelings. Using language that acknowledges and validates emotions, such as "I see that you are feeling sad" or "It sounds like you are really happy about that," helps children develop a vocabulary for expressing their emotions and fosters emotional intelligence.

Empathy is not just about understanding the emotions of others; it also involves taking compassionate action. Teaching children to care for others means encouraging them to engage in acts of kindness and generosity. This can be done through both everyday interactions and organized activities. Simple acts such as helping a friend with a task, sharing toys, or comforting someone who is upset are opportunities for children to practice empathy. Adults can reinforce these behaviors by praising and acknowledging the child's efforts to care for others.

Community service and volunteer activities are also powerful ways to cultivate empathy. Involving children in activities such as helping at a local food bank, visiting a nursing home, or participating in environmental clean-up projects can provide them with firsthand experience of the impact of their actions on others. These activities help children see the world beyond their immediate surroundings and develop a sense of responsibility and compassion for their community.

Modeling empathetic behavior is crucial for teaching children to care for others. Children learn by observing the actions of the adults around them. When parents and caregivers consistently demonstrate empathy in their interactions, children are more likely to adopt these behaviors themselves. This includes showing empathy towards the child, other family members, friends, and even strangers. For example, showing concern for a neighbor who is ill, expressing sympathy for a friend's loss, or offering help to someone in need are all ways to model empathetic behavior.

It is also important to create an environment that encourages empathy and discourages behaviors that undermine it. This involves setting clear expectations for behavior, providing consistent discipline, and addressing issues such as bullying and exclusion. Encouraging positive social interactions and teaching conflict resolution skills are essential for fostering a culture of empathy and respect.

Developing emotional regulation skills is another important aspect of building empathy. Children who are able to manage their own emotions are better equipped to understand and respond to the emotions of others. Teaching children techniques for calming themselves, such as deep breathing, counting to ten, or using positive self-talk, can help them regulate their emotions and respond empathetically in challenging situations. Mindfulness practices, such as guided meditation or mindful breathing exercises, can also help children develop greater emotional awareness and control.

In addition to these strategies, it is important to recognize and celebrate empathetic behavior. When children demonstrate empathy, whether through words or actions, acknowledging and praising their efforts reinforces the value of caring for others. This positive reinforcement encourages children to continue practicing empathy and helps them understand the importance of their actions.

Empathy is a skill that continues to develop throughout a person's life. As children grow and encounter new experiences, their understanding and capacity for empathy can deepen and expand.

Providing ongoing support and opportunities for practicing empathy is essential for nurturing this important trait. This includes engaging in regular conversations about emotions, encouraging children to reflect on their interactions with others, and providing guidance and support as they navigate social relationships.

In summary, building empathy in children is a multifaceted process that involves modeling empathetic behavior, providing opportunities for perspective-taking, encouraging compassionate actions, and fostering emotional regulation skills. By creating an environment that values and supports empathy, parents and caregivers can help children develop the ability to understand and care for the emotions and experiences of others. This not only enhances their social and emotional development but also contributes to the creation of a more compassionate and connected society. Through consistent practice and reinforcement, children can learn to embody empathy in their daily lives and carry this important trait into adulthood.

ᗞᗞᗞ

"Amidst the chaos, find your calm; within the
storm, discover your strength; for in adversity, lies
the seed of triumph."

❦❦❦

THREE

CULTIVATING RESPECT: INSTILLING APPRECIATION FOR SELF AND OTHERS

Cultivating respect in children is a foundational aspect of their character development and overall growth. Respect involves recognizing the inherent worth of oneself and others, treating people with kindness and consideration, and valuing diverse perspectives and experiences. Instilling respect in children requires a multifaceted approach that includes modeling respectful behavior, setting clear expectations, providing consistent discipline, and fostering an environment where respect is both taught and practiced.

From an early age, children observe and absorb the behaviors and attitudes of those around them. Parents and caregivers play a crucial role in modeling respect through their interactions with others. When adults demonstrate respectful behavior in their daily lives, children learn to emulate these actions. Simple gestures such as saying "please" and "thank you," listening attentively when someone is speaking, and showing appreciation for others' efforts can have a significant impact on a child's understanding of respect. These behaviors teach children that everyone deserves to be treated with kindness and consideration.

One of the most important aspects of cultivating respect is teaching children to respect themselves. Self-respect involves recognizing one's own worth, setting healthy boundaries, and taking care of one's physical and emotional well-being. When children have a strong sense of self-respect, they are more likely to treat others with respect as well. To foster self-respect, it is important for adults to create an environment where children feel valued and supported. This includes providing positive reinforcement, encouraging self-expression, and helping children develop a healthy self-image.

Setting clear expectations for behavior is essential for teaching respect. Children need to understand what is expected of them and why certain behaviors are important. Establishing rules and guidelines that promote respectful behavior helps children learn to navigate social interactions and understand the consequences of their actions. Consistent discipline is also crucial in reinforcing these expectations. When children understand that respectful behavior is consistently encouraged and valued, they are more likely to internalize these values and act accordingly.

Respect is not only about how we treat others but also about how we appreciate and value diverse perspectives and experiences. Encouraging children to be open-minded and empathetic helps them develop a deeper understanding of the world around them. This can be achieved by exposing children to different cultures, traditions, and viewpoints through books, stories, and discussions. Engaging in conversations about the importance of diversity and inclusion helps children appreciate the richness of different perspectives and fosters a sense of global citizenship.

Active listening is a key component of respectful behavior. When children learn to listen attentively to others, they show that they value and respect the thoughts and feelings of those around them. Teaching active listening skills involves encouraging children to make eye contact, avoid interrupting, and respond thoughtfully to what others are saying. Role-playing exercises and games that focus on listening and communication can help children practice and develop these skills in a fun and engaging way.

Encouraging empathy is another important aspect of cultivating respect. Empathy involves understanding and sharing the feelings of others, and it is essential for building strong, respectful relationships. Helping children develop empathy involves teaching them to recognize and validate the emotions of others, encouraging them to consider different perspectives, and providing opportunities for them to practice compassionate actions. Activities such as reading stories about diverse characters, discussing real-life scenarios, and participating in community service projects can help children develop a greater sense of empathy and respect for others.

Conflict resolution skills are also crucial for fostering respect. Conflicts are a natural part of human interactions, and teaching children how to resolve them respectfully is essential for maintaining healthy relationships. This involves helping children learn to express their feelings and needs in a constructive manner, actively listen to others, and work together to find mutually agreeable solutions. Role-playing conflict resolution scenarios and discussing different strategies for managing disagreements can help children develop the skills they need to navigate conflicts respectfully.

Providing children with opportunities to practice respectful behavior is essential for reinforcing these values. This can be done through both structured activities and everyday interactions. Encouraging children to participate in group activities, such as team sports or collaborative projects, helps them learn to work together, respect each other's contributions, and develop a sense of shared responsibility. Additionally, involving children in family decisions and chores helps them understand the importance of cooperation and respect within the household.

Positive reinforcement is a powerful tool for encouraging respectful behavior. When children receive praise and recognition for their respectful actions, they are more likely to continue exhibiting these behaviors. This can be as simple as acknowledging when a child shows kindness, listens attentively, or demonstrates empathy. Providing specific feedback about what the child did well helps them understand the importance of their actions and reinforces the value of respect.

It is also important to address disrespectful behavior in a constructive manner. When children act disrespectfully, it is an opportunity for learning and growth. Rather than simply punishing the behavior, adults should take the time to discuss why the behavior was inappropriate and how it affected others. This helps children understand the impact of their actions and learn how to make better choices in the future. Encouraging children to apologize and make amends when they have acted disrespectfully also helps them develop a sense of accountability and responsibility.

Fostering a sense of gratitude is another important aspect of cultivating respect. When children learn to appreciate the people, experiences, and things in their lives, they are more likely to treat others with respect and kindness. Encouraging children to express gratitude through practices such as keeping a gratitude journal, writing thank-you notes, or sharing what they are thankful for during family meals helps them develop a positive and appreciative mindset.

Creating an environment where respect is consistently practiced and valued is essential for nurturing respectful behavior in children. This involves setting a positive example, providing clear expectations, offering consistent discipline, and encouraging empathy and open-mindedness. By fostering a culture of respect within the home and community, adults can help children develop the values and skills they need to build healthy, respectful relationships and contribute positively to society.

Respect is a lifelong value that continues to grow and evolve as children develop. Providing ongoing support and guidance is essential for helping children navigate the complexities of social interactions and relationships. Engaging in regular conversations about respect, reflecting on personal experiences, and providing opportunities for children to practice and reinforce respectful behavior are all important aspects of this process.

Ultimately, cultivating respect in children is about helping them recognize the inherent worth of themselves and others, appreciate diverse perspectives and experiences, and treat people with kindness and consideration. By instilling these values from an early age and providing a supportive and nurturing environment, parents and caregivers can help children develop the skills and attitudes they need to lead respectful and fulfilling lives. Through consistent practice and reinforcement, children can learn to embody respect in their daily interactions and carry this important value into adulthood, contributing to a more compassionate and harmonious society.

❦❦❦

"To journey through darkness is to find the stars; to embrace failure is to unlock the door to success; for within every setback lies the seed of opportunity."

ᗐᗐᗐ

FOUR

Developing Honesty: Fostering Truthfulness in Everyday Life

Developing honesty in children is a vital part of their moral and ethical growth. Honesty, the quality of being truthful and transparent, is fundamental to building trust, fostering healthy relationships, and creating a society based on integrity and mutual respect. Fostering truthfulness in everyday life requires a multifaceted approach that includes modeling honest behavior, creating an environment where honesty is valued, and teaching children the importance and benefits of being truthful.

Children learn from observing the behaviors and attitudes of the adults around them. Parents and caregivers play a critical role in modeling honesty. When adults consistently demonstrate truthful behavior in their interactions, children are more likely to adopt these behaviors themselves. This includes being honest in both significant and everyday matters. For example, admitting mistakes, acknowledging when something is unknown, and providing truthful answers to children's questions all contribute to creating an environment where honesty is the norm.

Creating a safe and supportive environment where children feel comfortable telling the truth is crucial for fostering honesty. Children are more likely to be honest when they know they will not be harshly judged or punished for their mistakes. Encouraging open communication and creating a nonjudgmental space where children can express themselves freely helps build their confidence in being truthful. When children feel understood and supported, they are more likely to trust their caregivers and be honest about their thoughts, feelings, and actions.

Positive reinforcement is a powerful tool for encouraging honesty. Praising and acknowledging children when they tell the truth reinforces the value of honesty and encourages them to continue being truthful. It is important to provide specific feedback about why their honesty is appreciated, such as saying, "I appreciate you telling the truth, even though it was difficult." This helps children understand the significance of their actions and reinforces the positive behavior.

Teaching children the importance and benefits of honesty involves explaining how being truthful builds trust and strengthens relationships. Children need to understand that honesty is not just about avoiding punishment but also about creating a foundation of trust and respect. Discussions about the consequences of dishonesty, such as losing trust or causing harm to others, can help children see the broader impact of their actions. Using stories and examples from everyday life can illustrate the value of honesty and make the concept more relatable.

It is also important to address dishonesty in a constructive manner. When children lie or engage in dishonest behavior, it is an opportunity for learning and growth. Rather than simply punishing the behavior, adults should take the time to discuss why the behavior was inappropriate and how it affected others. This helps children understand the impact of their actions and learn how to make better choices in the future. Encouraging children to take responsibility for their actions, apologize, and make amends when they have been dishonest helps them develop a sense of accountability and integrity.

Role-playing and practicing honest communication can help children develop the skills they need to be truthful. Engaging in activities where children practice telling the truth, even in challenging situations, can build their confidence and competence in being honest. For example, role-playing scenarios where a child has to admit to a mistake or tell the truth about a difficult situation can help them practice and reinforce honest behavior in a supportive environment.

Consistency is key in fostering honesty. Children need to see that honesty is consistently valued and encouraged in all aspects of life. This includes being honest with themselves, their peers, and adults. By consistently promoting and reinforcing honest behavior, adults can help children internalize the value of honesty and make it a fundamental part of their character.

Helping children understand that honesty is not always easy but is always important is crucial for their moral development. Children may face situations where telling the truth is difficult or uncomfortable. It is important to support them in these moments and help them navigate the challenges of being honest. Encouraging children to consider the long-term benefits of honesty, such as building trust and maintaining integrity, can help them see the value in being truthful even when it is hard.

Teaching children to differentiate between honesty and tact is also important. While it is essential to be truthful, it is equally important to be considerate of others' feelings. Helping children understand how to communicate honestly but kindly can help them navigate social interactions more effectively. For example, teaching them to provide constructive feedback rather than hurtful criticism helps them learn to balance honesty with empathy and respect.

In addition to modeling and teaching honesty, it is important to create opportunities for children to practice and reinforce this value in their daily lives. Encouraging children to reflect on their experiences and discuss times when they were honest or faced challenges in being truthful can help reinforce the importance of honesty. Providing opportunities for children to engage in activities that promote honesty, such as group discussions, storytelling, and collaborative projects, helps them practice and develop this important value.

Creating a culture of honesty within the family and community is essential for fostering truthfulness. When honesty is consistently valued and reinforced in all aspects of life, children are more likely to internalize this value and make it a fundamental part of their character. This includes being honest in their interactions with peers, teachers, and other adults. By promoting a culture of honesty, adults can help children develop the skills and attitudes they need to lead lives based on integrity and mutual respect.

It is also important to recognize that developing honesty is a lifelong process. Children will continue to encounter new challenges and situations that test their commitment to being truthful. Providing ongoing support, guidance, and reinforcement is essential for helping children navigate these challenges and maintain their commitment to honesty. Engaging in regular conversations about honesty, reflecting on personal experiences, and providing opportunities for children to practice and reinforce honest behavior are all important aspects of this process.

Ultimately, developing honesty in children is about helping them recognize the value and importance of being truthful and transparent in their interactions with others. By modeling honest behavior, creating a supportive environment, and providing consistent reinforcement, parents and caregivers can help children develop the skills and attitudes they need to lead lives based on integrity and mutual respect. Through consistent practice and reinforcement, children can learn to embody honesty in their daily interactions and carry this important value into adulthood, contributing to a more trustworthy and harmonious society.

"The road less traveled may be fraught with challenges, but it is also adorned with the most breathtaking views."

ᘐᘐᘐ

FIVE

The Power of Kindness: Encouraging Acts of Compassion

The power of kindness cannot be overstated. Acts of compassion, no matter how small, have the potential to transform lives, build strong communities, and create a more empathetic and connected world. Encouraging kindness in children is crucial for their social and emotional development. By teaching children to be kind, we help them develop important skills such as empathy, cooperation, and emotional intelligence, which are essential for building healthy relationships and contributing positively to society.

From an early age, children are capable of understanding and exhibiting kindness. They learn about kindness through their interactions with parents, caregivers, and peers. One of the most effective ways to encourage kindness in children is by modeling compassionate behavior. When adults demonstrate acts of kindness in their daily lives, children observe and learn from these actions. Simple gestures such as helping a neighbor, expressing gratitude, or offering support to someone in need can have a profound impact on a child's understanding of kindness.

Creating an environment that fosters kindness is essential for nurturing compassionate behavior in children. This involves setting clear expectations for behavior, providing consistent reinforcement, and creating opportunities for children to practice kindness. When children know that kindness is valued and encouraged, they are more likely to adopt these behaviors themselves. Positive reinforcement, such as praising and acknowledging kind actions, helps reinforce the importance of kindness and encourages children to continue exhibiting compassionate behavior.

Teaching empathy is a key component of encouraging kindness. Empathy, the ability to understand and share the feelings of others, is essential for compassionate behavior. Helping children develop empathy involves teaching them to recognize and validate the emotions of others, encouraging them to consider different perspectives, and providing opportunities for them to practice empathetic actions. Activities such as reading stories about diverse characters, discussing real-life scenarios, and engaging in role-playing exercises can help children develop a greater sense of empathy and understanding.

Providing opportunities for children to engage in acts of kindness is crucial for reinforcing compassionate behavior. This can be done through both structured activities and everyday interactions. Encouraging children to participate in community service projects, such as volunteering at a local food bank, visiting a nursing home, or participating in environmental clean-up efforts, helps them see the impact of their actions and develop a sense of responsibility and compassion for their community. Additionally, everyday acts of kindness, such as helping a friend with a task, sharing toys, or comforting someone who is upset, provide opportunities for children to practice and reinforce kind behavior.

It is important to create a culture of kindness within the family and community. When kindness is consistently valued and reinforced in all aspects of life, children are more likely to internalize this value and make it a fundamental part of their character. This includes promoting kindness in interactions with peers, teachers, and other adults. By creating a culture of kindness, adults can help children develop the skills and attitudes they need to build strong, compassionate relationships and contribute positively to society.

Encouraging children to express gratitude is another important aspect of fostering kindness. Gratitude involves recognizing and appreciating the positive aspects of life and the contributions of others. When children learn to express gratitude, they develop a positive and appreciative mindset, which enhances their ability to be kind and compassionate. Practices such as keeping a gratitude journal, writing thank-you notes, or sharing what they are thankful for during family meals help children develop a sense of gratitude and appreciation.

Teaching children to be mindful of others' needs and feelings is essential for nurturing kindness. This involves encouraging them to be attentive and considerate of the people around them, and to think about how their actions affect others. Helping children develop good listening skills, encouraging them to ask questions and show interest in others, and teaching them to be considerate and thoughtful in their interactions all contribute to fostering a mindful and compassionate approach to life.

It is also important to help children understand that kindness is not always easy, but it is always important. There may be times when being kind requires effort, courage, or sacrifice. Teaching children to recognize these challenges and to persevere in their commitment to kindness, even when it is difficult, helps them develop resilience and strength of character. Encouraging children to reflect on the long-term benefits of kindness, such as building strong relationships and creating a positive impact on the world, can help them see the value in being compassionate and caring.

Creating opportunities for children to practice kindness in different contexts helps reinforce compassionate behavior and develop a well-rounded understanding of what it means to be kind. This can include participating in group activities, such as team sports or collaborative projects, where children learn to work together, respect each other's contributions, and develop a sense of shared responsibility. Additionally, involving children in family decisions and chores helps them understand the importance of cooperation and kindness within the household.

Positive reinforcement is a powerful tool for encouraging kindness. When children receive praise and recognition for their kind actions, they are more likely to continue exhibiting these behaviors. Providing specific feedback about what the child did well, such as saying, "I appreciate how you helped your friend when they were upset," helps them understand the significance of their actions and reinforces the value of kindness. Additionally, recognizing and celebrating acts of kindness within the family and community helps create a culture where compassionate behavior is valued and encouraged.

It is also important to address unkind behavior in a constructive manner. When children act unkindly, it is an opportunity for learning and growth. Rather than simply punishing the behavior, adults should take the time to discuss why the behavior was inappropriate and how it affected others. This helps children understand the impact of their actions and learn how to make better choices in the future. Encouraging children to apologize and make amends when they have acted unkindly helps them develop a sense of accountability and responsibility.

Fostering a sense of community and connectedness is essential for nurturing kindness. When children feel connected to their family, friends, and community, they are more likely to exhibit compassionate behavior. Encouraging children to build strong, positive relationships with others, participate in community activities, and develop a sense of belonging helps create a supportive environment where kindness can flourish.

Teaching children to be kind to themselves is also important for their overall well-being and ability to be compassionate to others. Self-compassion involves recognizing one's own worth, treating oneself with kindness and understanding, and taking care of one's physical and emotional needs. When children learn to be kind to themselves, they develop a positive self-image and a greater capacity for empathy and kindness towards others. Encouraging children to practice self-care, recognize their strengths, and treat themselves with kindness helps foster a healthy sense of self-compassion.

Encouraging kindness is a lifelong process. Children will continue to encounter new challenges and situations that test their commitment to being compassionate and caring. Providing ongoing support, guidance, and reinforcement is essential for helping children navigate these challenges and maintain their commitment to kindness. Engaging in regular conversations about kindness, reflecting on personal experiences, and providing opportunities for children to practice and reinforce kind behavior are all important aspects of this process.

Ultimately, the power of kindness lies in its ability to create positive change in the world. By encouraging acts of compassion in children, we help them develop the skills and attitudes they need to build strong, empathetic relationships and contribute positively to society. Through consistent practice and reinforcement, children can learn to embody kindness in their daily interactions and carry this important value into adulthood, creating a more compassionate and connected world for all.

ᐅᐅᐅ

"In the tapestry of existence, every thread is essential; for it is the imperfections that render it truly magnificent."

❦❦❦

SIX

RESPONSIBILITY MATTERS: HELPING KIDS TAKE OWNERSHIP OF THEIR ACTIONS

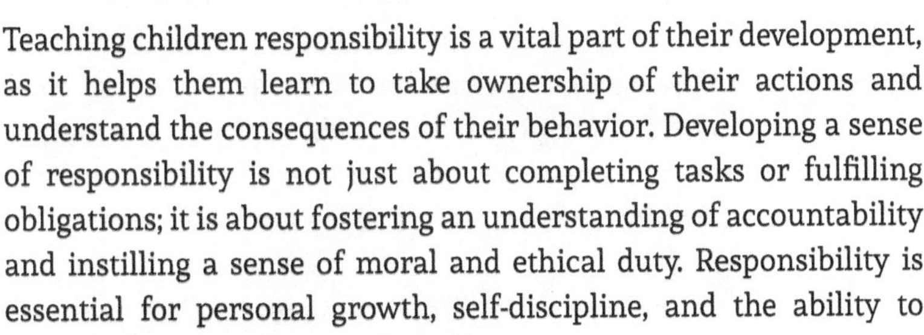

Teaching children responsibility is a vital part of their development, as it helps them learn to take ownership of their actions and understand the consequences of their behavior. Developing a sense of responsibility is not just about completing tasks or fulfilling obligations; it is about fostering an understanding of accountability and instilling a sense of moral and ethical duty. Responsibility is essential for personal growth, self-discipline, and the ability to navigate life's challenges effectively.

From a young age, children can be taught the value of responsibility through simple, age-appropriate tasks and expectations. These tasks help them understand that their actions have consequences and that they play an important role in their family, community, and the world around them. Parents and caregivers play a crucial role in this process by modeling responsible behavior, setting clear expectations, providing consistent discipline, and offering guidance and support.

Modeling responsible behavior is one of the most effective ways to teach children about responsibility. Children learn by observing the actions and attitudes of the adults around them. When parents and caregivers consistently demonstrate responsible behavior, such as fulfilling their commitments, being reliable, and taking ownership of their actions, children are more likely to adopt these behaviors themselves. This includes everyday actions like being punctual, keeping promises, and completing tasks on time. By showing children what responsible behavior looks like, adults can help them develop a clear understanding of what it means to be responsible.

Setting clear expectations is essential for helping children understand their responsibilities. Children need to know what is expected of them and why certain behaviors are important. Establishing rules and guidelines that promote responsible behavior helps children learn to navigate their daily lives and understand the importance of fulfilling their obligations. This includes tasks such as completing homework, doing household chores, and following through on commitments. Providing clear instructions and explaining the reasons behind these expectations helps children understand the value of responsibility and the impact of their actions on themselves and others.

Consistent discipline is crucial in reinforcing responsible behavior. When children understand that there are consistent consequences for their actions, they are more likely to take ownership of their behavior and make responsible choices. This does not mean punishing children harshly, but rather providing appropriate consequences that help them learn from their mistakes and understand the importance of responsibility. For example, if a child forgets to complete a homework assignment, a natural consequence might be losing some free time to finish the task. By providing consistent and fair consequences, parents and caregivers can help children develop a sense of accountability and learn to take responsibility for their actions.

Guidance and support are essential for helping children develop responsibility. Children need to know that they are not alone in their efforts to become responsible individuals. Providing support and encouragement helps children feel confident in their abilities and motivates them to take ownership of their actions. This includes offering help when needed, providing positive reinforcement for responsible behavior, and being available to discuss challenges and successes. By offering guidance and support, parents and caregivers can help children navigate the complexities of responsibility and develop the skills they need to be successful.

Teaching children to take ownership of their actions involves helping them understand the connection between their choices and the outcomes of those choices. This includes encouraging children to think about the consequences of their actions and how their behavior affects themselves and others. Discussing real-life scenarios and asking questions such as "What do you think will happen if you don't complete your homework?" or "How do you think your actions made your friend feel?" helps children develop a deeper understanding of accountability and responsibility. By encouraging children to reflect on their actions and consider the impact of their behavior, parents and caregivers can help them develop a strong sense of responsibility.

Providing opportunities for children to practice responsibility is crucial for reinforcing this value. This can be done through both structured activities and everyday interactions. Encouraging children to take on age-appropriate tasks and responsibilities, such as caring for a pet, managing their own schoolwork, or helping with household chores, helps them develop a sense of ownership and accountability. Additionally, involving children in family decisions and discussions about responsibilities helps them understand the importance of cooperation and shared responsibility within the household.

Positive reinforcement is a powerful tool for encouraging responsible behavior. When children receive praise and recognition for their responsible actions, they are more likely to continue exhibiting these behaviors. Providing specific feedback about what the child did well, such as saying, "I appreciate how you took care of your chores without being reminded," helps them understand the significance of their actions and reinforces the value of responsibility. Additionally, recognizing and celebrating responsible behavior within the family and community helps create a culture where accountability and responsibility are valued and encouraged.

Helping children develop problem-solving skills is also important for fostering responsibility. When children learn to identify problems, think critically about solutions, and take action to resolve issues, they develop a sense of ownership and accountability. Encouraging children to brainstorm solutions to challenges, make decisions, and evaluate the outcomes of their actions helps them build the skills they need to take responsibility for their behavior. This includes teaching children to learn from their mistakes and view challenges as opportunities for growth and learning.

Creating a sense of community and connectedness is essential for nurturing responsibility. When children feel connected to their family, friends, and community, they are more likely to exhibit responsible behavior. Encouraging children to build strong, positive relationships with others, participate in community activities, and develop a sense of belonging helps create a supportive environment where responsibility can flourish. Additionally, teaching children about their responsibilities to others and the importance of contributing to the well-being of their community helps them develop a broader understanding of accountability and responsibility.

Teaching children to be responsible also involves helping them develop self-discipline and time management skills. Self-discipline is the ability to control one's impulses and behaviors, while time management involves effectively organizing and prioritizing tasks. Both skills are essential for taking responsibility and achieving long-term goals. Encouraging children to set goals, create schedules, and manage their time effectively helps them develop the self-discipline and organizational skills they need to fulfill their responsibilities. Additionally, teaching children techniques for staying focused and avoiding distractions, such as breaking tasks into smaller steps or setting specific times for work and play, helps them develop the skills they need to take ownership of their actions.

Responsibility is a lifelong value that continues to grow and evolve as children develop. Providing ongoing support, guidance, and reinforcement is essential for helping children navigate the complexities of responsibility and maintain their commitment to accountability. Engaging in regular conversations about responsibility, reflecting on personal experiences, and providing opportunities for children to practice and reinforce responsible behavior are all important aspects of this process.

Ultimately, teaching children responsibility is about helping them recognize the importance of taking ownership of their actions and understanding the impact of their behavior on themselves and others. By modeling responsible behavior, setting clear expectations, providing consistent discipline, and offering guidance and support, parents and caregivers can help children develop the skills and attitudes they need to lead lives based on accountability and mutual respect. Through consistent practice and reinforcement, children can learn to embody responsibility in their daily interactions and carry this important value into adulthood, contributing to a more reliable and trustworthy society.

ひひひ

"Courage is not the absence of fear, but the audacity
to persist in the face of it."

ᐅᐅᐅ

SEVEN

Instilling Courage: Encouraging Bravery in Facing Challenges

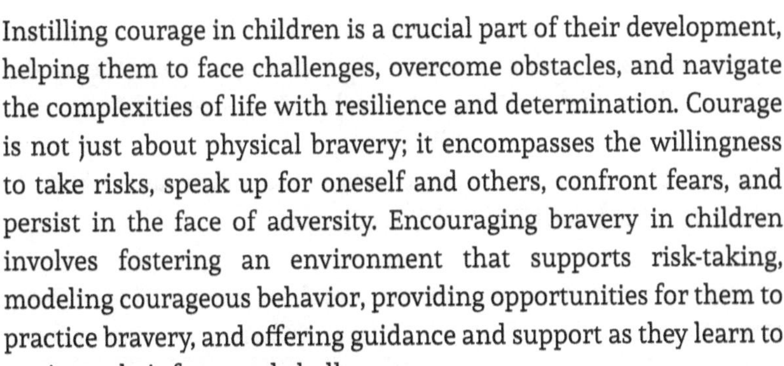

Instilling courage in children is a crucial part of their development, helping them to face challenges, overcome obstacles, and navigate the complexities of life with resilience and determination. Courage is not just about physical bravery; it encompasses the willingness to take risks, speak up for oneself and others, confront fears, and persist in the face of adversity. Encouraging bravery in children involves fostering an environment that supports risk-taking, modeling courageous behavior, providing opportunities for them to practice bravery, and offering guidance and support as they learn to navigate their fears and challenges.

From a young age, children begin to encounter situations that require courage. Whether it's trying a new activity, standing up to a bully, or admitting a mistake, these experiences shape their ability to handle fear and uncertainty. Parents and caregivers play a vital role in helping children develop courage by creating a safe and supportive environment where they feel valued and understood. This involves acknowledging their fears, validating their feelings, and encouraging them to face challenges with confidence and determination.

Modeling courageous behavior is one of the most effective ways to teach children about bravery. Children learn by observing the actions and attitudes of the adults around them. When parents and caregivers demonstrate courage in their own lives, children are more likely to adopt these behaviors themselves. This includes everyday actions such as trying new things, speaking up for what is right, and persevering in the face of difficulties. By showing children what courage looks like, adults can help them develop a clear understanding of what it means to be brave.

Creating an environment that supports risk-taking is essential for fostering courage. Children need to know that it's okay to make mistakes and that failure is a natural part of learning and growth. Encouraging children to take risks and try new things helps them build confidence and resilience. This involves providing opportunities for them to explore their interests, experiment with new activities, and challenge themselves in a safe and supportive setting. Celebrating their efforts, rather than just their successes, helps reinforce the value of courage and encourages them to continue taking risks and facing challenges.

Positive reinforcement is a powerful tool for encouraging bravery. Praising and acknowledging children when they demonstrate courage helps reinforce the importance of bravery and motivates them to continue being courageous. Providing specific feedback about what the child did well, such as saying, "I admire how you stood up for your friend," helps them understand the significance of their actions and reinforces the positive behavior. Additionally, recognizing and celebrating acts of bravery within the family and community helps create a culture where courage is valued and encouraged.

Helping children develop a growth mindset is also important for fostering courage. A growth mindset is the belief that abilities and intelligence can be developed through effort and perseverance. Encouraging children to view challenges as opportunities for growth, rather than as threats, helps them develop the resilience and determination they need to face difficulties with courage. This involves teaching children to embrace challenges, learn from their mistakes, and persist in the face of setbacks. By fostering a growth mindset, parents and caregivers can help children develop the confidence and resilience they need to be brave.

Teaching children to manage their fears is essential for helping them develop courage. Fear is a natural and normal response to uncertainty and danger, but it can become a barrier to action if not managed effectively. Helping children understand and manage their fears involves teaching them coping strategies, such as deep breathing, positive self-talk, and visualization techniques. Encouraging children to talk about their fears and providing reassurance and support helps them feel understood and supported. By teaching children to manage their fears, parents and caregivers can help them develop the confidence and resilience they need to face challenges with courage.

Providing opportunities for children to practice bravery is crucial for reinforcing this value. This can be done through both structured activities and everyday interactions. Encouraging children to take on age-appropriate challenges, such as trying a new sport, speaking in front of a group, or solving a difficult problem, helps them develop a sense of confidence and competence. Additionally, involving children in family decisions and discussions about challenges helps them understand the importance of courage and the impact of their actions on themselves and others.

Encouraging children to advocate for themselves and others is an important aspect of fostering courage. This involves teaching them to speak up for their needs and rights, as well as standing up for others who may be facing difficulties. Helping children develop assertiveness skills, such as expressing their opinions and setting boundaries, empowers them to take action and face challenges with confidence. By encouraging children to advocate for themselves and others, parents and caregivers can help them develop the courage to stand up for what is right and make a positive impact in their communities.

Teaching children to persevere in the face of difficulties is essential for helping them develop courage. Perseverance involves continuing to pursue a goal or overcome a challenge despite obstacles and setbacks. Encouraging children to set goals, break tasks into manageable steps, and persist in their efforts helps them develop the resilience and determination they need to be brave. Celebrating their efforts and progress, rather than just their achievements, helps reinforce the value of perseverance and encourages them to continue facing challenges with courage.

Helping children develop problem-solving skills is also important for fostering courage. When children learn to identify problems, think critically about solutions, and take action to resolve issues, they develop a sense of confidence and competence. Encouraging children to brainstorm solutions to challenges, make decisions, and evaluate the outcomes of their actions helps them build the skills they need to face difficulties with courage. This includes teaching children to learn from their mistakes and view challenges as opportunities for growth and learning.

Creating a sense of community and connectedness is essential for nurturing courage. When children feel connected to their family, friends, and community, they are more likely to exhibit courageous behavior. Encouraging children to build strong, positive relationships with others, participate in community activities, and develop a sense of belonging helps create a supportive environment where courage can flourish. Additionally, teaching children about their responsibilities to others and the importance of contributing to the well-being of their community helps them develop a broader understanding of courage and the impact of their actions on the world around them.

Encouraging children to be kind to themselves is also important for their overall well-being and ability to be courageous. Self-compassion involves recognizing one's own worth, treating oneself with kindness and understanding, and taking care of one's physical and emotional needs. When children learn to be kind to themselves, they develop a positive self-image and a greater capacity for resilience and courage. Encouraging children to practice self-care, recognize their strengths, and treat themselves with kindness helps foster a healthy sense of self-compassion.

Courage is a lifelong value that continues to grow and evolve as children develop. Providing ongoing support, guidance, and reinforcement is essential for helping children navigate the complexities of courage and maintain their commitment to bravery. Engaging in regular conversations about courage, reflecting on personal experiences, and providing opportunities for children to practice and reinforce courageous behavior are all important aspects of this process.

Ultimately, instilling courage in children is about helping them recognize the importance of facing challenges, overcoming obstacles, and taking risks with confidence and determination. By modeling courageous behavior, creating a supportive environment, and providing consistent reinforcement, parents and caregivers can help children develop the skills and attitudes they need to lead lives based on bravery and resilience. Through consistent practice and reinforcement, children can learn to embody courage in their daily interactions and carry this important value into adulthood, contributing to a more confident and resilient society.

ᐅᐅᐅ

"To dream is to defy gravity, to soar amidst the clouds of possibility, and to paint the sky with the colors of imagination."

ppp

EIGHT

THE VALUE OF PATIENCE: TEACHING THE ART OF WAITING

The value of patience is often underestimated in a fast-paced world where instant gratification is the norm. Teaching children the art of waiting is essential for their emotional and social development. Patience involves the ability to endure delays, tolerate frustration, and stay calm under pressure. It is a critical skill that helps children develop self-control, resilience, and the capacity to deal with life's inevitable challenges. Cultivating patience in children requires a multifaceted approach that includes modeling patient behavior, creating opportunities for them to practice waiting, and providing guidance and support to help them navigate situations that test their patience.

Children begin to encounter situations that require patience from a very young age. Whether it's waiting for their turn to play, standing in line, or delaying gratification for a desired reward, these experiences shape their ability to manage their impulses and emotions. Parents and caregivers play a crucial role in helping children develop patience by creating an environment that encourages waiting, providing consistent reinforcement, and modeling calm and patient behavior.

Modeling patient behavior is one of the most effective ways to teach children about patience. Children learn by observing the actions and attitudes of the adults around them. When parents and caregivers consistently demonstrate patience in their own lives, children are more likely to adopt these behaviors themselves. This includes everyday actions such as waiting calmly in traffic, handling delays with composure, and responding to frustrating situations with a positive attitude. By showing children what patience looks like, adults can help them develop a clear understanding of the importance of waiting and staying calm under pressure.

Creating an environment that supports patience is essential for fostering this value in children. This involves setting clear expectations for behavior, providing consistent discipline, and creating opportunities for children to practice waiting. When children know that waiting is expected and valued, they are more likely to develop the skills needed to be patient. Positive reinforcement, such as praising and acknowledging patient behavior, helps reinforce the importance of patience and encourages children to continue practicing it. For example, saying, "I appreciate how you waited your turn without complaining," provides specific feedback that helps children understand the significance of their actions.

Teaching children to delay gratification is a key component of developing patience. Delaying gratification involves postponing immediate rewards for greater benefits in the future. Helping children understand the value of waiting for something worthwhile is essential for their long-term success and well-being. This can be done through activities such as saving money for a desired toy, waiting for a special treat, or working towards a long-term goal. By encouraging children to delay gratification, parents and caregivers can help them develop the self-control and perseverance needed to achieve their goals and manage their impulses.

Providing opportunities for children to practice patience is crucial for reinforcing this value. This can be done through both structured activities and everyday interactions. Engaging children in activities that require waiting, such as playing board games, gardening, or cooking, helps them develop the skills needed to be patient. Additionally, involving children in family routines that involve waiting, such as waiting for everyone to be seated before eating or taking turns during conversations, helps them understand the importance of patience in daily life.

Teaching children to manage their emotions is essential for helping them develop patience. Patience requires the ability to stay calm and composed in the face of delays and frustrations. Helping children understand and manage their emotions involves teaching them coping strategies, such as deep breathing, positive self-talk, and mindfulness techniques. Encouraging children to talk about their feelings and providing reassurance and support helps them feel understood and supported. By teaching children to manage their emotions, parents and caregivers can help them develop the self-control and resilience needed to be patient.

Positive reinforcement is a powerful tool for encouraging patience. When children receive praise and recognition for their patient behavior, they are more likely to continue exhibiting these behaviors. Providing specific feedback about what the child did well, such as saying, "I admire how you waited calmly for your turn," helps them understand the significance of their actions and reinforces the positive behavior. Additionally, recognizing and celebrating patient behavior within the family and community helps create a culture where patience is valued and encouraged.

Helping children develop problem-solving skills is also important for fostering patience. When children learn to identify problems, think critically about solutions, and take action to resolve issues, they develop a sense of confidence and competence. Encouraging children to brainstorm solutions to challenges, make decisions, and evaluate the outcomes of their actions helps them build the skills they need to manage delays and frustrations with patience. This includes teaching children to learn from their mistakes and view challenges as opportunities for growth and learning.

Creating a sense of community and connectedness is essential for nurturing patience. When children feel connected to their family, friends, and community, they are more likely to exhibit patient behavior. Encouraging children to build strong, positive relationships with others, participate in community activities, and develop a sense of belonging helps create a supportive environment where patience can flourish. Additionally, teaching children about their responsibilities to others and the importance of contributing to the well-being of their community helps them develop a broader understanding of patience and the impact of their actions on the world around them.

Encouraging children to be kind to themselves is also important for their overall well-being and ability to be patient. Self-compassion involves recognizing one's own worth, treating oneself with kindness and understanding, and taking care of one's physical and emotional needs. When children learn to be kind to themselves, they develop a positive self-image and a greater capacity for resilience and patience. Encouraging children to practice self-care, recognize their strengths, and treat themselves with kindness helps foster a healthy sense of self-compassion.

Patience is a lifelong value that continues to grow and evolve as children develop. Providing ongoing support, guidance, and reinforcement is essential for helping children navigate the complexities of patience and maintain their commitment to waiting and staying calm under pressure. Engaging in regular conversations about patience, reflecting on personal experiences, and providing opportunities for children to practice and reinforce patient behavior are all important aspects of this process.

Ultimately, teaching children the value of patience is about helping them recognize the importance of waiting, enduring delays, and staying calm under pressure. By modeling patient behavior, creating a supportive environment, and providing consistent reinforcement, parents and caregivers can help children develop the skills and attitudes they need to lead lives based on self-control and resilience. Through consistent practice and reinforcement, children can learn to embody patience in their daily interactions and carry this important value into adulthood, contributing to a more composed and understanding society.

ppp

"In the dance of life, embrace both the light and the shadows, for it is the contrast that unveils the true beauty of the journey."

♥♥♥

NINE

Promoting Gratitude: Nurturing Thankfulness in Young Hearts

Promoting gratitude in children is a fundamental aspect of nurturing their emotional and social development. Gratitude, the practice of recognizing and appreciating the positive aspects of life, enhances well-being, fosters positive relationships, and contributes to a more compassionate and connected society. Teaching children to be thankful helps them develop a positive outlook on life, build resilience, and cultivate a sense of contentment. Encouraging gratitude involves modeling thankful behavior, creating opportunities for children to practice gratitude, and providing guidance and support to help them develop a grateful mindset.

Children begin to understand and express gratitude from a young age. Parents and caregivers play a crucial role in helping children develop this important value by creating an environment that encourages thankfulness, providing consistent reinforcement, and modeling grateful behavior. When children see adults consistently demonstrating gratitude, they are more likely to adopt these behaviors themselves. This includes everyday actions such as saying "thank you," acknowledging the efforts of others, and expressing appreciation for the good things in life. By showing children what gratitude looks like, adults can help them develop a clear understanding of the importance of being thankful.

Creating an environment that supports gratitude is essential for fostering this value in children. This involves setting clear expectations for behavior, providing consistent discipline, and creating opportunities for children to practice thankfulness. When children know that gratitude is expected and valued, they are more likely to develop the skills needed to be thankful. Positive reinforcement, such as praising and acknowledging grateful behavior, helps reinforce the importance of gratitude and encourages children to continue practicing it. For example, saying, "I appreciate how you thanked your friend for helping you," provides specific feedback that helps children understand the significance of their actions.

Encouraging children to express gratitude involves teaching them to recognize and appreciate the positive aspects of their lives. This can be done through activities such as keeping a gratitude journal, where children write down things they are thankful for each day, or creating a gratitude jar, where they can place notes of appreciation for the good things that happen. These practices help children develop a habit of focusing on the positive and expressing their gratitude regularly. Additionally, encouraging children to express their thankfulness through actions, such as writing thank-you notes, giving compliments, or performing acts of kindness, helps them understand the impact of their gratitude on others.

Teaching children to appreciate the efforts of others is an important aspect of promoting gratitude. This involves helping children understand that many aspects of their lives are made possible through the efforts and contributions of others. Encouraging children to acknowledge and thank the people who help and support them, such as family members, teachers, friends, and community workers, helps them develop a deeper sense of appreciation and gratitude. This can be done through simple actions like saying thank you, writing notes of appreciation, or giving small tokens of gratitude.

Helping children develop empathy is also crucial for fostering gratitude. Empathy, the ability to understand and share the feelings of others, enhances their ability to appreciate the efforts and contributions of others. Teaching children to consider the perspectives of others, recognize their feelings, and understand the impact of their actions helps them develop a greater sense of gratitude and appreciation. Activities such as reading stories about diverse characters, discussing real-life scenarios, and engaging in role-playing exercises can help children develop empathy and a deeper sense of gratitude.

Positive reinforcement is a powerful tool for encouraging gratitude. When children receive praise and recognition for their grateful behavior, they are more likely to continue exhibiting these behaviors. Providing specific feedback about what the child did well, such as saying, "I admire how you thanked your friend for sharing their toy," helps them understand the significance of their actions and reinforces the positive behavior. Additionally, recognizing and celebrating grateful behavior within the family and community helps create a culture where gratitude is valued and encouraged.

Teaching children to manage their emotions is essential for helping them develop gratitude. Gratitude requires the ability to recognize and appreciate the positive aspects of life, even in the face of challenges and setbacks. Helping children understand and manage their emotions involves teaching them coping strategies, such as deep breathing, positive self-talk, and mindfulness techniques. Encouraging children to talk about their feelings and providing reassurance and support helps them feel understood and supported. By teaching children to manage their emotions, parents and caregivers can help them develop the resilience and positive outlook needed to be grateful.

Providing opportunities for children to practice gratitude is crucial for reinforcing this value. This can be done through both structured activities and everyday interactions. Engaging children in activities that promote thankfulness, such as volunteering, participating in community service projects, or helping others, helps them develop a sense of responsibility and appreciation for the contributions of others. Additionally, involving children in family routines that encourage gratitude, such as sharing things they are thankful for during family meals or expressing appreciation for each other's efforts, helps them understand the importance of gratitude in daily life.

Helping children develop a growth mindset is also important for fostering gratitude. A growth mindset is the belief that abilities and intelligence can be developed through effort and perseverance. Encouraging children to view challenges as opportunities for growth, rather than as threats, helps them develop the resilience and positive outlook needed to be grateful. This involves teaching children to embrace challenges, learn from their mistakes, and persist in the face of setbacks. By fostering a growth mindset, parents and caregivers can help children develop the confidence and resilience they need to be grateful.

Creating a sense of community and connectedness is essential for nurturing gratitude. When children feel connected to their family, friends, and community, they are more likely to exhibit grateful behavior. Encouraging children to build strong, positive relationships with others, participate in community activities, and develop a sense of belonging helps create a supportive environment where gratitude can flourish. Additionally, teaching children about their responsibilities to others and the importance of contributing to the well-being of their community helps them develop a broader understanding of gratitude and the impact of their actions on the world around them.

Encouraging children to be kind to themselves is also important for their overall well-being and ability to be grateful. Self-compassion involves recognizing one's own worth, treating oneself with kindness and understanding, and taking care of one's physical and emotional needs. When children learn to be kind to themselves, they develop a positive self-image and a greater capacity for resilience and gratitude. Encouraging children to practice self-care, recognize their strengths, and treat themselves with kindness helps foster a healthy sense of self-compassion.

Gratitude is a lifelong value that continues to grow and evolve as children develop. Providing ongoing support, guidance, and reinforcement is essential for helping children navigate the complexities of gratitude and maintain their commitment to being thankful. Engaging in regular conversations about gratitude, reflecting on personal experiences, and providing opportunities for children to practice and reinforce grateful behavior are all important aspects of this process.

Ultimately, promoting gratitude in children is about helping them recognize the importance of being thankful for the positive aspects of their lives and the contributions of others. By modeling grateful behavior, creating a supportive environment, and providing consistent reinforcement, parents and caregivers can help children develop the skills and attitudes they need to lead lives based on gratitude and appreciation. Through consistent practice and reinforcement, children can learn to embody gratitude in their daily interactions and carry this important value into adulthood, contributing to a more compassionate and connected society.

❥❥❥

"Like a phoenix rising from the ashes, adversity
ignites the flames of resilience, birthing strength
from the embers of struggle."

ᗡᗡᗡ

TEN

THE IMPORTANCE OF HUMILITY: BALANCING SELF-ESTEEM WITH MODESTY

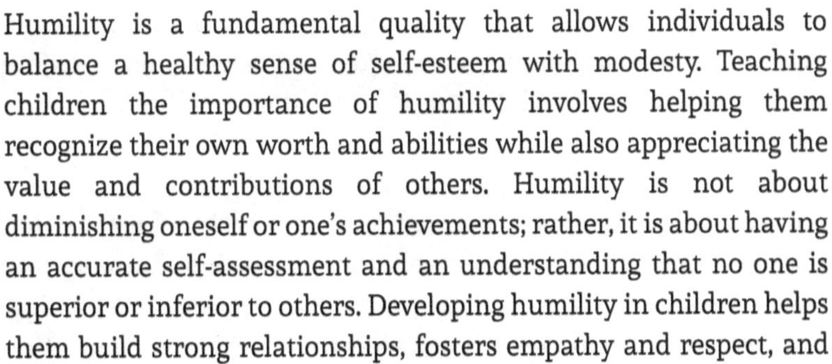

Humility is a fundamental quality that allows individuals to balance a healthy sense of self-esteem with modesty. Teaching children the importance of humility involves helping them recognize their own worth and abilities while also appreciating the value and contributions of others. Humility is not about diminishing oneself or one's achievements; rather, it is about having an accurate self-assessment and an understanding that no one is superior or inferior to others. Developing humility in children helps them build strong relationships, fosters empathy and respect, and contributes to their overall personal growth and well-being.

From a young age, children begin to form an understanding of their abilities and strengths. Encouraging a healthy self-esteem is crucial for their development, but it must be balanced with humility to prevent arrogance and entitlement. Parents and caregivers play a pivotal role in modeling humble behavior, setting realistic expectations, and providing guidance to help children appreciate their own talents while recognizing and valuing the contributions of others.

Modeling humble behavior is one of the most effective ways to teach children about humility. Children learn by observing the actions and attitudes of the adults around them. When parents and caregivers consistently demonstrate humility in their interactions, children are more likely to adopt these behaviors themselves.

This includes acknowledging one's limitations, giving credit to others, and showing appreciation for the support and efforts of others. By exhibiting humility, adults can help children understand the importance of being modest and appreciative, even when they achieve success or receive praise.

Creating an environment that supports humility is essential for fostering this value in children. This involves setting clear expectations for behavior, providing consistent discipline, and creating opportunities for children to practice humility. When children know that humility is expected and valued, they are more likely to develop the skills needed to balance self-esteem with modesty.

Positive reinforcement, such as praising and acknowledging humble behavior, helps reinforce the importance of humility and encourages children to continue practicing it. For example, saying, "I appreciate how you recognized your friend's help in completing the project," provides specific feedback that helps children understand the significance of their actions.

Encouraging children to reflect on their achievements and

recognize the contributions of others is a key component of developing humility. This can be done through activities such as discussing team projects, acknowledging the efforts of classmates, or reflecting on the support received from family members.

By helping children understand that their successes are often the result of collaborative efforts and the support of others, parents and caregivers can foster a sense of appreciation and humility. Teaching children to express gratitude for the help and support they receive reinforces the value of humility and helps them develop a balanced sense of self-esteem.

Helping children develop empathy is also crucial for fostering humility. Empathy, the ability to understand and share the feelings of others, enhances their ability to appreciate the experiences and contributions of others. Teaching children to consider the perspectives of others, recognize their feelings, and understand the impact of their actions helps them develop a greater sense of humility and respect.

Activities such as reading stories about diverse characters, discussing real-life scenarios, and engaging in role-playing exercises can help children develop empathy and a deeper sense of humility.

Positive reinforcement is a powerful tool for encouraging humility. When children receive praise and recognition for their humble behavior, they are more likely to continue exhibiting these behaviors. Providing specific feedback about what the child did well, such as saying, "I admire how you gave credit to your team for the success of the project," helps them understand the significance of their actions and reinforces the positive behavior.

Additionally, recognizing and celebrating humble behavior within the family and community helps create a culture where humility is valued and encouraged.

Teaching children to manage their ego is essential for helping them develop humility. Ego, the sense of self-importance, can sometimes overshadow humility and lead to arrogance. Helping children understand and manage their ego involves teaching them coping strategies, such as deep breathing, positive self-talk, and mindfulness techniques.

Encouraging children to talk about their feelings and providing reassurance and support helps them feel understood and supported. By teaching children to manage their ego, parents and caregivers can help them develop the self-control and awareness needed to be humble.

Providing opportunities for children to practice humility is crucial for reinforcing this value. This can be done through both structured activities and everyday interactions. Engaging children in activities that promote teamwork, collaboration, and mutual respect helps them develop the skills needed to be humble. Additionally, involving children in family routines that encourage humility, such as sharing responsibilities, acknowledging each other's efforts, and expressing gratitude, helps them understand the importance of humility in daily life.

Helping children develop a growth mindset is also important for fostering humility. A growth mindset is the belief that abilities and intelligence can be developed through effort and perseverance. Encouraging children to view challenges as opportunities for growth, rather than as threats, helps them develop the resilience and positive outlook needed to be humble.

This involves teaching children to embrace challenges, learn from their mistakes, and persist in the face of setbacks. By fostering a growth mindset, parents and caregivers can help children develop the confidence and humility they need to recognize their own abilities while appreciating the efforts of others.

Creating a sense of community and connectedness is essential for nurturing humility. When children feel connected to their family, friends, and community, they are more likely to exhibit humble behavior. Encouraging children to build strong, positive relationships with others, participate in community activities, and develop a sense of belonging helps create a supportive environment where humility can flourish.

Additionally, teaching children about their responsibilities to others and the importance of contributing to the well-being of their community helps them develop a broader understanding of humility and the impact of their actions on the world around them.

Encouraging children to be kind to themselves is also important for their overall well-being and ability to be humble. Self-compassion involves recognizing one's own worth, treating oneself with kindness and understanding, and taking care of one's physical and emotional needs. When children learn to be kind to themselves, they develop a positive self-image and a greater capacity for resilience and humility. Encouraging children to practice self-care, recognize their strengths, and treat themselves with kindness helps foster a healthy sense of self-compassion.

Humility is a lifelong value that continues to grow and evolve as children develop. Providing ongoing support, guidance, and reinforcement is essential for helping children navigate the complexities of humility and maintain their commitment to balancing self-esteem with modesty.

Engaging in regular conversations about humility, reflecting on personal experiences, and providing opportunities for children to practice and reinforce humble behavior are all important aspects of this process.

Ultimately, teaching children the importance of humility is about helping them recognize the value of balancing a healthy sense of self-esteem with modesty. By modeling humble behavior, creating a supportive environment, and providing consistent reinforcement, parents and caregivers can help children develop the skills and attitudes they need to lead lives based on humility and respect.

Through consistent practice and reinforcement, children can learn to embody humility in their daily interactions and carry this important value into adulthood, contributing to a more compassionate and connected society.

ᗺᗺᗺ

"In the garden of life, adversity is the fertilizer that
nourishes the seeds of growth, yielding the most
vibrant blooms."

♥♥♥

ELEVEN

FOSTERING GENEROSITY: ENCOURAGING GIVING AND SHARING

Fostering generosity in children is a critical aspect of their emotional and social development. Generosity, the willingness to give and share without expecting anything in return, is a quality that enhances social connections, promotes empathy, and contributes to a more compassionate and cohesive society. Encouraging children to be generous involves teaching them the value of giving, modeling generous behavior, creating opportunities for them to practice generosity, and providing guidance and support to help them develop a giving spirit.

From an early age, children can begin to understand the concept of sharing and giving. Parents and caregivers play a vital role in helping children develop this important value by creating an environment that encourages generosity, providing consistent reinforcement, and modeling giving behavior. When children see adults consistently demonstrating generosity in their interactions, they are more likely to adopt these behaviors themselves. This includes everyday actions such as sharing resources, offering help, and giving without expecting anything in return. By showing children what generosity looks like, adults can help them develop a clear understanding of the importance of giving and sharing.

Creating an environment that supports generosity is essential for fostering this value in children. This involves setting clear expectations for behavior, providing consistent discipline, and creating opportunities for children to practice giving and sharing. When children know that generosity is expected and valued, they are more likely to develop the skills needed to be giving. Positive reinforcement, such as praising and acknowledging generous behavior, helps reinforce the importance of generosity and encourages children to continue practicing it. For example, saying, "I appreciate how you shared your toy with your friend," provides specific feedback that helps children understand the significance of their actions.

Encouraging children to engage in acts of kindness and giving is a key component of developing generosity. This can be done through activities such as donating toys and clothes to those in need, volunteering at local charities, or participating in community service projects. By involving children in acts of giving, parents and caregivers can help them understand the impact of their generosity on others and develop a sense of responsibility and compassion. Teaching children to give their time, effort, and resources to help others fosters a sense of community and connectedness and reinforces the value of generosity.

Helping children develop empathy is also crucial for fostering generosity. Empathy, the ability to understand and share the feelings of others, enhances their ability to appreciate the needs and experiences of others. Teaching children to consider the perspectives of others, recognize their feelings, and understand the impact of their actions helps them develop a greater sense of empathy and a giving spirit. Activities such as reading stories about diverse characters, discussing real-life scenarios, and engaging in role-playing exercises can help children develop empathy and a deeper sense of generosity.

Positive reinforcement is a powerful tool for encouraging generosity. When children receive praise and recognition for their generous behavior, they are more likely to continue exhibiting these behaviors. Providing specific feedback about what the child did well, such as saying, "I admire how you helped your classmate with their homework," helps them understand the significance of their actions and reinforces the positive behavior. Additionally, recognizing and celebrating generous behavior within the family and community helps create a culture where giving is valued and encouraged.

Teaching children to manage their desires and impulses is essential for helping them develop generosity. Generosity requires the ability to prioritize the needs of others and give without expecting anything in return. Helping children understand and manage their desires involves teaching them coping strategies, such as deep breathing, positive self-talk, and mindfulness techniques. Encouraging children to talk about their feelings and providing reassurance and support helps them feel understood and supported. By teaching children to manage their desires, parents and caregivers can help them develop the self-control and awareness needed to be generous.

Providing opportunities for children to practice generosity is crucial for reinforcing this value. This can be done through both structured activities and everyday interactions. Encouraging children to share their toys, help others, and participate in charitable activities helps them develop the skills needed to be giving. Additionally, involving children in family routines that encourage generosity, such as donating to charity, volunteering, or helping neighbors, helps them understand the importance of giving and sharing in daily life.

Helping children develop a growth mindset is also important for fostering generosity. A growth mindset is the belief that abilities and intelligence can be developed through effort and perseverance. Encouraging children to view challenges as opportunities for growth, rather than as threats, helps them develop the resilience and positive outlook needed to be generous. This involves teaching children to embrace challenges, learn from their mistakes, and persist in the face of setbacks. By fostering a growth mindset, parents and caregivers can help children develop the confidence and generosity they need to recognize their own abilities while appreciating the efforts of others.

Creating a sense of community and connectedness is essential for nurturing generosity. When children feel connected to their family, friends, and community, they are more likely to exhibit generous behavior. Encouraging children to build strong, positive relationships with others, participate in community activities, and develop a sense of belonging helps create a supportive environment where generosity can flourish. Additionally, teaching children about their responsibilities to others and the importance of contributing to the well-being of their community helps them develop a broader understanding of generosity and the impact of their actions on the world around them.

Encouraging children to be kind to themselves is also important for their overall well-being and ability to be generous. Self-compassion involves recognizing one's own worth, treating oneself with kindness and understanding, and taking care of one's physical and emotional needs. When children learn to be kind to themselves, they develop a positive self-image and a greater capacity for resilience and generosity. Encouraging children to practice self-care, recognize their strengths, and treat themselves with kindness helps foster a healthy sense of self-compassion.

Generosity is a lifelong value that continues to grow and evolve as children develop. Providing ongoing support, guidance, and reinforcement is essential for helping children navigate the complexities of generosity and maintain their commitment to giving and sharing. Engaging in regular conversations about generosity, reflecting on personal experiences, and providing opportunities for children to practice and reinforce generous behavior are all important aspects of this process.

Ultimately, fostering generosity in children is about helping them recognize the importance of giving and sharing without expecting anything in return. By modeling generous behavior, creating a supportive environment, and providing consistent reinforcement, parents and caregivers can help children develop the skills and attitudes they need to lead lives based on generosity and compassion. Through consistent practice and reinforcement, children can learn to embody generosity in their daily interactions and carry this important value into adulthood, contributing to a more compassionate and connected society.

ᏊᏊᏊ

"Within the confines of fear lies the key to
liberation; for it is only by facing our fears that we
discover our truest selves."

♥♥♥

TWELVE

Nurturing Self-Discipline: Helping Kids Control Their Impulses

Nurturing self-discipline in children is essential for their personal growth, academic success, and overall well-being. Self-discipline, the ability to control impulses and delay gratification, enables children to make thoughtful decisions, set and achieve goals, and navigate challenges effectively. Helping children develop self-discipline involves creating a supportive environment, modeling disciplined behavior, teaching practical strategies for impulse control, and providing consistent guidance and reinforcement.

Children begin to encounter situations that require self-discipline from an early age. Whether it's waiting for their turn to speak, resisting the temptation to eat sweets before dinner, or focusing on homework instead of playing, these experiences shape their ability to manage their impulses and make responsible choices. Parents and caregivers play a crucial role in helping children develop self-discipline by setting clear expectations, providing consistent discipline, and offering guidance and support.

Modeling disciplined behavior is one of the most effective ways to teach children about self-discipline. Children learn by observing the actions and attitudes of the adults around them. When parents and caregivers consistently demonstrate self-discipline in their own lives, children are more likely to adopt these behaviors themselves.

This includes everyday actions such as sticking to routines, following through on commitments, and managing time effectively. By showing children what self-discipline looks like, adults can help them develop a clear understanding of the importance of controlling impulses and making thoughtful decisions.

Creating an environment that supports self-discipline is essential for fostering this value in children. This involves setting clear expectations for behavior, providing consistent discipline, and creating opportunities for children to practice self-control. When children know that self-discipline is expected and valued, they are more likely to develop the skills needed to manage their impulses.

Positive reinforcement, such as praising and acknowledging disciplined behavior, helps reinforce the importance of self-discipline and encourages children to continue practicing it. For example, saying, "I appreciate how you waited patiently for your turn," provides specific feedback that helps children understand the significance of their actions.

Teaching children to delay gratification is a key component of developing self-discipline. Delaying gratification involves postponing immediate rewards for greater benefits in the future. Helping children understand the value of waiting for something worthwhile is essential for their long-term success and well-being.

This can be done through activities such as saving money for a desired toy, waiting for a special treat, or working towards a long-term goal. By encouraging children to delay gratification, parents and caregivers can help them develop the self-control and perseverance needed to achieve their goals and manage their impulses.

Providing opportunities for children to practice self-discipline is crucial for reinforcing this value. This can be done through both structured activities and everyday interactions. Engaging children in activities that require self-control, such as playing games with rules, completing tasks before playing, or following routines, helps them develop the skills needed to manage their impulses.

Additionally, involving children in family routines that encourage self-discipline, such as setting and following schedules, planning and preparing meals, and completing chores, helps them understand the importance of self-discipline in daily life.

Helping children develop a growth mindset is also important for fostering self-discipline. A growth mindset is the belief that abilities and intelligence can be developed through effort and perseverance. Encouraging children to view challenges as opportunities for growth, rather than as threats, helps them develop the resilience and positive outlook needed to practice self-discipline.

This involves teaching children to embrace challenges, learn from their mistakes, and persist in the face of setbacks. By fostering a growth mindset, parents and caregivers can help children develop the confidence and self-discipline they need to recognize their own abilities while appreciating the efforts of others.

Teaching children to manage their emotions is essential for helping them develop self-discipline. Self-discipline requires the ability to stay calm and composed in the face of temptations and frustrations. Helping children understand and manage their emotions involves teaching them coping strategies, such as deep breathing, positive self-talk, and mindfulness techniques.

Encouraging children to talk about their feelings and providing reassurance and support helps them feel understood and supported. By teaching children to manage their emotions, parents and caregivers can help them develop the self-control and resilience needed to practice self-discipline.

Positive reinforcement is a powerful tool for encouraging self-discipline. When children receive praise and recognition for their disciplined behavior, they are more likely to continue exhibiting these behaviors. Providing specific feedback about what the child did well, such as saying, "I admire how you focused on your homework before playing," helps them understand the significance of their actions and reinforces the positive behavior.

Additionally, recognizing and celebrating disciplined behavior within the family and community helps create a culture where self-discipline is valued and encouraged.

Helping children develop problem-solving skills is also important for fostering self-discipline. When children learn to identify problems, think critically about solutions, and take action to resolve issues, they develop a sense of confidence and competence. Encouraging children to brainstorm solutions to challenges, make decisions, and evaluate the outcomes of their actions helps them build the skills they need to manage impulses and make responsible choices. This includes teaching children to learn from their mistakes and view challenges as opportunities for growth and learning.

Creating a sense of community and connectedness is essential for nurturing self-discipline. When children feel connected to their family, friends, and community, they are more likely to exhibit disciplined behavior. Encouraging children to build strong, positive relationships with others, participate in community activities, and develop a sense of belonging helps create a supportive environment where self-discipline can flourish.

Additionally, teaching children about their responsibilities to others and the importance of contributing to the well-being of their community helps them develop a broader understanding of self-discipline and the impact of their actions on the world around them.

Encouraging children to be kind to themselves is also important for their overall well-being and ability to practice self-discipline. Self-compassion involves recognizing one's own worth, treating oneself with kindness and understanding, and taking care of one's physical and emotional needs.

When children learn to be kind to themselves, they develop a positive self-image and a greater capacity for resilience and self-discipline. Encouraging children to practice self-care, recognize their strengths, and treat themselves with kindness helps foster a healthy sense of self-compassion.

Self-discipline is a lifelong value that continues to grow and evolve as children develop. Providing ongoing support, guidance, and reinforcement is essential for helping children navigate the complexities of self-discipline and maintain their commitment to controlling their impulses.

Engaging in regular conversations about self-discipline, reflecting on personal experiences, and providing opportunities for children to practice and reinforce disciplined behavior are all important aspects of this process.

Ultimately, nurturing self-discipline in children is about helping them recognize the importance of controlling their impulses and making thoughtful decisions. By modeling disciplined behavior, creating a supportive environment, and providing consistent reinforcement, parents and caregivers can help children develop the skills and attitudes they need to lead lives based on self-control and responsibility.

Through consistent practice and reinforcement, children can learn to embody self-discipline in their daily interactions and carry this important value into adulthood, contributing to a more responsible and resilient society.

"To traverse the path of uncertainty is to sculpt
one's destiny from the raw marble of possibility,
chiseling away doubt to reveal the masterpiece
within."

ppp

THIRTEEN

THE ROLE OF PERSEVERANCE: TEACHING PERSISTENCE AND DETERMINATION

Perseverance is a vital quality that enables individuals to pursue their goals despite difficulties and setbacks. Teaching children the role of perseverance is essential for their personal development, academic success, and overall resilience. Perseverance involves persistence and determination, the ability to keep going even when faced with challenges.

It helps children develop a strong work ethic, enhances their problem-solving skills, and fosters a positive mindset. Encouraging perseverance in children requires a comprehensive approach that includes modeling persistent behavior, creating opportunities for them to practice perseverance, and providing consistent guidance and support.

From a young age, children encounter situations that test their perseverance. Whether it's learning to tie their shoes, completing a difficult puzzle, or mastering a new skill, these experiences shape their ability to persist in the face of obstacles. Parents and caregivers play a crucial role in helping children develop perseverance by creating an environment that supports persistence, providing consistent reinforcement, and modeling determined behavior.

When children see adults consistently demonstrating perseverance, they are more likely to adopt these behaviors themselves. This includes everyday actions such as tackling challenging tasks, staying focused on long-term goals, and not giving up easily. By showing children what perseverance looks like, adults can help them develop a clear understanding of the importance of persistence and determination.

Creating an environment that supports perseverance is essential for fostering this value in children. This involves setting clear expectations for behavior, providing consistent discipline, and creating opportunities for children to practice persistence. When children know that perseverance is expected and valued, they are more likely to develop the skills needed to persist in the face of difficulties.

Positive reinforcement, such as praising and acknowledging persistent behavior, helps reinforce the importance of perseverance and encourages children to continue practicing it. For example, saying, "I appreciate how you kept trying even when the task was difficult," provides specific feedback that helps children understand the significance of their actions.

Encouraging children to set and work towards goals is a key component of developing perseverance. Goal-setting helps children understand the importance of persistence and determination in achieving their aspirations. This can be done through activities such as creating vision boards, setting short-term and long-term goals, and breaking tasks into manageable steps.

By encouraging children to set goals and work towards them, parents and caregivers can help them develop the persistence and determination needed to achieve their dreams. Teaching children to celebrate their progress and accomplishments along the way also reinforces the value of perseverance and motivates them to continue striving towards their goals.

Providing opportunities for children to practice perseverance is crucial for reinforcing this value. This can be done through both structured activities and everyday interactions. Engaging children in activities that require persistence, such as sports, music lessons, or academic challenges, helps them develop the skills needed to persist in the face of difficulties.

Additionally, involving children in family routines that encourage perseverance, such as completing chores, working on projects, or participating in group activities, helps them understand the importance of persistence and determination in daily life.

Helping children develop a growth mindset is also important for fostering perseverance. A growth mindset is the belief that abilities and intelligence can be developed through effort and perseverance. Encouraging children to view challenges as opportunities for growth, rather than as threats, helps them develop the resilience and positive outlook needed to practice perseverance.

This involves teaching children to embrace challenges, learn from their mistakes, and persist in the face of setbacks. By fostering a growth mindset, parents and caregivers can help children develop the confidence and perseverance they need to recognize their own abilities while appreciating the efforts of others.

Teaching children to manage their emotions is essential for helping them develop perseverance. Perseverance requires the ability to stay calm and composed in the face of difficulties and frustrations. Helping children understand and manage their emotions involves teaching them coping strategies, such as deep breathing, positive self-talk, and mindfulness techniques.

Encouraging children to talk about their feelings and providing reassurance and support helps them feel understood and supported. By teaching children to manage their emotions, parents and caregivers can help them develop the resilience and persistence needed to practice perseverance.

Positive reinforcement is a powerful tool for encouraging perseverance. When children receive praise and recognition for their persistent behavior, they are more likely to continue exhibiting these behaviors. Providing specific feedback about what the child did well, such as saying, "I admire how you kept working on your project even when it was challenging," helps them understand the significance of their actions and reinforces the positive behavior.

Additionally, recognizing and celebrating persistent behavior within the family and community helps create a culture where perseverance is valued and encouraged.

Helping children develop problem-solving skills is also important for fostering perseverance. When children learn to identify problems, think critically about solutions, and take action to resolve issues, they develop a sense of confidence and competence. Encouraging children to brainstorm solutions to challenges, make decisions, and evaluate the outcomes of their actions helps them build the skills they need to persist in the face of difficulties and make responsible choices. This includes teaching children to learn from their mistakes and view challenges as opportunities for growth and learning.

Creating a sense of community and connectedness is essential for nurturing perseverance. When children feel connected to their family, friends, and community, they are more likely to exhibit persistent behavior. Encouraging children to build strong, positive relationships with others, participate in community activities, and develop a sense of belonging helps create a supportive environment where perseverance can flourish.

Additionally, teaching children about their responsibilities to others and the importance of contributing to the well-being of their community helps them develop a broader understanding of perseverance and the impact of their actions on the world around them.

Encouraging children to be kind to themselves is also important for their overall well-being and ability to practice perseverance. Self-compassion involves recognizing one's own worth, treating oneself with kindness and understanding, and taking care of one's physical and emotional needs.

When children learn to be kind to themselves, they develop a positive self-image and a greater capacity for resilience and perseverance. Encouraging children to practice self-care, recognize their strengths, and treat themselves with kindness helps foster a healthy sense of self-compassion.

Perseverance is a lifelong value that continues to grow and evolve as children develop. Providing ongoing support, guidance, and reinforcement is essential for helping children navigate the complexities of perseverance and maintain their commitment to persistence and determination. Engaging in regular conversations about perseverance, reflecting on personal experiences, and providing opportunities for children to practice and reinforce persistent behavior are all important aspects of this process.

Ultimately, teaching children the role of perseverance is about helping them recognize the importance of persistence and determination in achieving their goals and overcoming challenges. By modeling persistent behavior, creating a supportive environment, and providing consistent reinforcement, parents and caregivers can help children develop the skills and attitudes they need to lead lives based on perseverance and resilience.

Through consistent practice and reinforcement, children can learn to embody perseverance in their daily interactions and carry this important value into adulthood, contributing to a more resilient and determined society.

ᐅᐅᐅ

"Embrace the storms that rage within, for it is in
their fury that the seeds of transformation are
sown, birthing new beginnings from the wreckage
of the old."

♡♡♡

FOURTEEN

ENCOURAGING OPTIMISM: PROMOTING A POSITIVE OUTLOOK ON LIFE

Encouraging optimism in children is a fundamental aspect of their emotional and psychological development. Optimism, the tendency to expect positive outcomes and maintain a hopeful outlook, significantly influences a child's ability to cope with challenges, build resilience, and achieve success. Promoting a positive outlook on life involves creating a supportive environment, modeling optimistic behavior, teaching practical strategies for maintaining a positive mindset, and providing consistent guidance and reinforcement.

Children begin to form their perspectives on life from a very young age. Parents and caregivers play a crucial role in shaping these perspectives by creating an environment that supports optimism, providing consistent reinforcement, and modeling positive behavior. When children see adults consistently demonstrating optimism in their interactions, they are more likely to adopt these attitudes themselves. This includes everyday actions such as maintaining a positive attitude in the face of setbacks, focusing on solutions rather than problems, and expressing gratitude for the good things in life. By showing children what optimism looks like, adults can help them develop a clear understanding of the importance of maintaining a hopeful and positive outlook.

Creating an environment that supports optimism is essential for fostering this value in children. This involves setting clear expectations for behavior, providing consistent discipline, and creating opportunities for children to practice positive thinking. When children know that optimism is expected and valued, they are more likely to develop the skills needed to maintain a positive outlook. Positive reinforcement, such as praising and acknowledging optimistic behavior, helps reinforce the importance of optimism and encourages children to continue practicing it. For example, saying, "I appreciate how you stayed positive and looked for solutions," provides specific feedback that helps children understand the significance of their actions.

Encouraging children to focus on the positive aspects of their lives is a key component of developing optimism. This can be done through activities such as keeping a gratitude journal, where children write down things they are thankful for each day, or creating a positive experiences jar, where they can place notes about good things that happen. These practices help children develop a habit of focusing on the positive and expressing their gratitude regularly. Additionally, encouraging children to express their optimism through actions, such as giving compliments, sharing good news, or performing acts of kindness, helps them understand the impact of their positive outlook on others.

Teaching children to reframe negative situations is also crucial for fostering optimism. Reframing involves looking at a situation from a different perspective and finding the positive aspects or potential benefits. Helping children develop this skill involves teaching them to ask questions such as, "What can I learn from this?" or "How can I turn this situation around?" By encouraging children to reframe negative situations, parents and caregivers can help them develop the resilience and positive outlook needed to cope with challenges and setbacks.

Positive reinforcement is a powerful tool for encouraging optimism. When children receive praise and recognition for their positive behavior, they are more likely to continue exhibiting these behaviors. Providing specific feedback about what the child did well, such as saying, "I admire how you found the good in a difficult situation," helps them understand the significance of their actions and reinforces the positive behavior. Additionally, recognizing and celebrating optimistic behavior within the family and community helps create a culture where a positive outlook is valued and encouraged.

Teaching children to manage their emotions is essential for helping them develop optimism. Optimism requires the ability to stay positive and hopeful in the face of challenges and frustrations. Helping children understand and manage their emotions involves teaching them coping strategies, such as deep breathing, positive self-talk, and mindfulness techniques. Encouraging children to talk about their feelings and providing reassurance and support helps them feel understood and supported. By teaching children to manage their emotions, parents and caregivers can help them develop the resilience and positive outlook needed to maintain optimism.

Providing opportunities for children to practice optimism is crucial for reinforcing this value. This can be done through both structured activities and everyday interactions. Engaging children in activities that promote positive thinking, such as setting and working towards goals, participating in positive affirmations, or practicing visualization techniques, helps them develop the skills needed to maintain a hopeful outlook. Additionally, involving children in family routines that encourage optimism, such as sharing positive moments during family meals or discussing what went well each day, helps them understand the importance of a positive outlook in daily life.

Helping children develop a growth mindset is also important for fostering optimism. A growth mindset is the belief that abilities and intelligence can be developed through effort and perseverance. Encouraging children to view challenges as opportunities for growth, rather than as threats, helps them develop the resilience and positive outlook needed to practice optimism. This involves teaching children to embrace challenges, learn from their mistakes, and persist in the face of setbacks. By fostering a growth mindset, parents and caregivers can help children develop the confidence and optimism they need to recognize their own abilities while appreciating the efforts of others.

Creating a sense of community and connectedness is essential for nurturing optimism. When children feel connected to their family, friends, and community, they are more likely to exhibit a positive outlook. Encouraging children to build strong, positive relationships with others, participate in community activities, and develop a sense of belonging helps create a supportive environment where optimism can flourish. Additionally, teaching children about their responsibilities to others and the importance of contributing to the well-being of their community helps them develop a broader understanding of optimism and the impact of their actions on the world around them.

Encouraging children to be kind to themselves is also important for their overall well-being and ability to practice optimism. Self-compassion involves recognizing one's own worth, treating oneself with kindness and understanding, and taking care of one's physical and emotional needs. When children learn to be kind to themselves, they develop a positive self-image and a greater capacity for resilience and optimism. Encouraging children to practice self-care, recognize their strengths, and treat themselves with kindness helps foster a healthy sense of self-compassion.

Optimism is a lifelong value that continues to grow and evolve as children develop. Providing ongoing support, guidance, and reinforcement is essential for helping children navigate the complexities of optimism and maintain their commitment to a positive outlook. Engaging in regular conversations about optimism, reflecting on personal experiences, and providing opportunities for children to practice and reinforce positive behavior are all important aspects of this process.

Ultimately, encouraging optimism in children is about helping them recognize the importance of maintaining a positive outlook on life. By modeling optimistic behavior, creating a supportive environment, and providing consistent reinforcement, parents and caregivers can help children develop the skills and attitudes they need to lead lives based on optimism and resilience. Through consistent practice and reinforcement, children can learn to embody optimism in their daily interactions and carry this important value into adulthood, contributing to a more hopeful and positive society.

ᐯᐯᐯ

"Like a compass in the wilderness, intuition guides
us through the labyrinth of life, whispering truths
amidst the cacophony of doubt."

ᛈᛈᛈ

FIFTEEN

THE JOY OF SERVICE: ENGAGING CHILDREN IN HELPING OTHERS

Engaging children in helping others is a powerful way to foster their personal development, build their sense of empathy, and instill a lifelong commitment to service. The joy of service is found in the profound satisfaction and fulfillment that comes from making a positive impact on the lives of others. Teaching children the value of service involves creating opportunities for them to participate in acts of kindness, modeling selfless behavior, and providing consistent guidance and reinforcement. By nurturing a spirit of service in children, we help them develop a deeper understanding of community, compassion, and responsibility.

From a young age, children can be introduced to the concept of helping others. Parents and caregivers play a crucial role in shaping children's attitudes toward service by creating an environment that encourages giving, providing consistent reinforcement, and modeling selfless behavior. When children see adults consistently engaging in acts of service, they are more likely to adopt these behaviors themselves. This includes everyday actions such as helping a neighbor, volunteering for community projects, and offering support to those in need. By showing children what service looks like, adults can help them develop a clear understanding of the importance of helping others and the joy that comes from making a positive difference.

Creating an environment that supports service is essential for fostering this value in children. This involves setting clear expectations for behavior, providing consistent discipline, and creating opportunities for children to participate in service activities. When children know that service is expected and valued, they are more likely to develop the skills needed to engage in helping others. Positive reinforcement, such as praising and acknowledging acts of service, helps reinforce the importance of service and encourages children to continue practicing it. For example, saying, "I appreciate how you helped clean up the park," provides specific feedback that helps children understand the significance of their actions.

Encouraging children to participate in service projects is a key component of developing a spirit of service. This can be done through activities such as volunteering at local charities, participating in community clean-up events, or organizing donation drives. By involving children in acts of service, parents and caregivers can help them understand the impact of their contributions and develop a sense of responsibility and compassion. Teaching children to give their time, effort, and resources to help others fosters a sense of community and connectedness and reinforces the value of service.

Helping children develop empathy is also crucial for fostering a spirit of service. Empathy, the ability to understand and share the feelings of others, enhances their ability to appreciate the needs and experiences of others. Teaching children to consider the perspectives of others, recognize their feelings, and understand the impact of their actions helps them develop a greater sense of empathy and a commitment to service. Activities such as reading stories about diverse characters, discussing real-life scenarios, and engaging in role-playing exercises can help children develop empathy and a deeper understanding of the importance of helping others.

Positive reinforcement is a powerful tool for encouraging service. When children receive praise and recognition for their acts of service, they are more likely to continue exhibiting these behaviors. Providing specific feedback about what the child did well, such as saying, "I admire how you volunteered to help at the shelter," helps them understand the significance of their actions and reinforces the positive behavior. Additionally, recognizing and celebrating acts of service within the family and community helps create a culture where helping others is valued and encouraged.

Teaching children to manage their desires and impulses is essential for helping them develop a spirit of service. Service requires the ability to prioritize the needs of others and give without expecting anything in return. Helping children understand and manage their desires involves teaching them coping strategies, such as deep breathing, positive self-talk, and mindfulness techniques. Encouraging children to talk about their feelings and providing reassurance and support helps them feel understood and supported. By teaching children to manage their desires, parents and caregivers can help them develop the self-control and awareness needed to engage in acts of service.

Providing opportunities for children to practice service is crucial for reinforcing this value. This can be done through both structured activities and everyday interactions. Encouraging children to share their toys, help others, and participate in charitable activities helps them develop the skills needed to engage in service. Additionally, involving children in family routines that encourage service, such as donating to charity, volunteering, or helping neighbors, helps them understand the importance of helping others in daily life.

Helping children develop a growth mindset is also important for fostering a spirit of service. A growth mindset is the belief that abilities and intelligence can be developed through effort and perseverance. Encouraging children to view challenges as opportunities for growth, rather than as threats, helps them develop the resilience and positive outlook needed to engage in service. This involves teaching children to embrace challenges, learn from their mistakes, and persist in the face of setbacks. By fostering a growth mindset, parents and caregivers can help children develop the confidence and commitment needed to recognize their own abilities while appreciating the efforts of others.

Creating a sense of community and connectedness is essential for nurturing a spirit of service. When children feel connected to their family, friends, and community, they are more likely to exhibit a commitment to helping others. Encouraging children to build strong, positive relationships with others, participate in community activities, and develop a sense of belonging helps create a supportive environment where service can flourish. Additionally, teaching children about their responsibilities to others and the importance of contributing to the well-being of their community helps them develop a broader understanding of service and the impact of their actions on the world around them.

Encouraging children to be kind to themselves is also important for their overall well-being and ability to engage in service. Self-compassion involves recognizing one's own worth, treating oneself with kindness and understanding, and taking care of one's physical and emotional needs. When children learn to be kind to themselves, they develop a positive self-image and a greater capacity for resilience and service. Encouraging children to practice self-care, recognize their strengths, and treat themselves with kindness helps foster a healthy sense of self-compassion.

Service is a lifelong value that continues to grow and evolve as children develop. Providing ongoing support, guidance, and reinforcement is essential for helping children navigate the complexities of service and maintain their commitment to helping others. Engaging in regular conversations about service, reflecting on personal experiences, and providing opportunities for children to practice and reinforce acts of service are all important aspects of this process.

Ultimately, engaging children in helping others is about helping them recognize the importance of making a positive impact on the lives of others. By modeling selfless behavior, creating a supportive environment, and providing consistent reinforcement, parents and caregivers can help children develop the skills and attitudes they need to lead lives based on service and compassion. Through consistent practice and reinforcement, children can learn to embody the joy of service in their daily interactions and carry this important value into adulthood, contributing to a more compassionate and connected society. The sense of fulfillment and joy that comes from helping others not only enriches the lives of those who receive help but also deeply enhances the lives of those who give, creating a cycle of kindness and generosity that benefits everyone involved.

ppp

"In the silence of solitude, listen closely; for it is in
the whispers of the soul that the universe reveals its
deepest secrets."

ᛈᛈᛈ

SIXTEEN

CULTIVATING FAIRNESS: UNDERSTANDING EQUALITY AND JUSTICE

Cultivating a sense of fairness in children is crucial for their development as empathetic, ethical, and socially responsible individuals. Fairness, encompassing the principles of equality and justice, helps children understand the importance of treating everyone with respect and dignity. Teaching fairness involves creating an environment where these values are consistently modeled, providing opportunities for children to practice fair behavior, and offering guidance and reinforcement to help them understand the importance of equality and justice.

Children begin to develop their sense of fairness at a young age, often through their interactions with siblings, peers, and adults. Parents and caregivers play a vital role in shaping children's understanding of fairness by modeling just behavior, setting clear expectations, and providing consistent discipline. When children see adults consistently demonstrating fairness in their interactions, they are more likely to adopt these behaviors themselves. This includes everyday actions such as sharing, taking turns, and listening to others' perspectives. By showing children what fairness looks like, adults can help them develop a clear understanding of the importance of equality and justice.

Creating an environment that supports fairness is essential for fostering this value in children. This involves setting clear expectations for behavior, providing consistent discipline, and creating opportunities for children to practice fair behavior. When children know that fairness is expected and valued, they are more likely to develop the skills needed to treat others with respect and justice. Positive reinforcement, such as praising and acknowledging fair behavior, helps reinforce the importance of fairness and encourages children to continue practicing it. For example, saying, "I appreciate how you shared your toys with your friends," provides specific feedback that helps children understand the significance of their actions.

Encouraging children to think about the perspectives of others is a key component of developing a sense of fairness. This can be done through activities such as role-playing, reading stories about diverse characters, and discussing real-life scenarios. By helping children understand the experiences and feelings of others, parents and caregivers can foster empathy and a deeper understanding of fairness. Teaching children to ask questions such as, "How would I feel if I were in that situation?" or "What can I do to make this situation fair for everyone?" encourages them to consider different perspectives and make decisions based on principles of equality and justice.

Helping children develop conflict resolution skills is also crucial for fostering fairness. Conflicts are a natural part of human interactions, and teaching children how to resolve them fairly is essential for maintaining healthy relationships. This involves helping children learn to express their feelings and needs constructively, listen to others, and work together to find mutually agreeable solutions. By teaching children to navigate conflicts with fairness and respect, parents and caregivers can help them develop the skills needed to maintain equitable and just relationships throughout their lives.

Positive reinforcement is a powerful tool for encouraging fairness. When children receive praise and recognition for their fair behavior, they are more likely to continue exhibiting these behaviors. Providing specific feedback about what the child did well, such as saying, "I admire how you included everyone in the game," helps them understand the significance of their actions and reinforces the positive behavior. Additionally, recognizing and celebrating fair behavior within the family and community helps create a culture where equality and justice are valued and encouraged.

Teaching children to manage their emotions is essential for helping them develop fairness. Fairness requires the ability to stay calm and composed in the face of conflicts and frustrations. Helping children understand and manage their emotions involves teaching them coping strategies, such as deep breathing, positive self-talk, and mindfulness techniques. Encouraging children to talk about their feelings and providing reassurance and support helps them feel understood and supported. By teaching children to manage their emotions, parents and caregivers can help them develop the self-control and empathy needed to practice fairness.

Providing opportunities for children to practice fairness is crucial for reinforcing this value. This can be done through both structured activities and everyday interactions. Encouraging children to participate in group activities, share responsibilities, and take turns helps them develop the skills needed to treat others with respect and justice. Additionally, involving children in family routines that encourage fairness, such as distributing chores equally, making decisions together, and listening to everyone's opinions, helps them understand the importance of equality and justice in daily life.

Helping children develop a growth mindset is also important for fostering fairness. A growth mindset is the belief that abilities and intelligence can be developed through effort and perseverance. Encouraging children to view challenges as opportunities for growth, rather than as threats, helps them develop the resilience and positive outlook needed to practice fairness. This involves teaching children to embrace challenges, learn from their mistakes, and persist in the face of setbacks. By fostering a growth mindset, parents and caregivers can help children develop the confidence and fairness they need to recognize their own abilities while appreciating the efforts of others.

Creating a sense of community and connectedness is essential for nurturing fairness. When children feel connected to their family, friends, and community, they are more likely to exhibit fair behavior. Encouraging children to build strong, positive relationships with others, participate in community activities, and develop a sense of belonging helps create a supportive environment where fairness can flourish. Additionally, teaching children about their responsibilities to others and the importance of contributing to the well-being of their community helps them develop a broader understanding of fairness and the impact of their actions on the world around them.

Encouraging children to be kind to themselves is also important for their overall well-being and ability to practice fairness. Self-compassion involves recognizing one's own worth, treating oneself with kindness and understanding, and taking care of one's physical and emotional needs. When children learn to be kind to themselves, they develop a positive self-image and a greater capacity for resilience and fairness. Encouraging children to practice self-care, recognize their strengths, and treat themselves with kindness helps foster a healthy sense of self-compassion.

Fairness is a lifelong value that continues to grow and evolve as children develop. Providing ongoing support, guidance, and reinforcement is essential for helping children navigate the complexities of fairness and maintain their commitment to equality and justice. Engaging in regular conversations about fairness, reflecting on personal experiences, and providing opportunities for children to practice and reinforce fair behavior are all important aspects of this process.

Ultimately, cultivating fairness in children is about helping them recognize the importance of treating everyone with respect and dignity. By modeling just behavior, creating a supportive environment, and providing consistent reinforcement, parents and caregivers can help children develop the skills and attitudes they need to lead lives based on fairness and empathy. Through consistent practice and reinforcement, children can learn to embody fairness in their daily interactions and carry this important value into adulthood, contributing to a more just and equitable society. The principles of equality and justice not only enrich the lives of those who practice them but also create a ripple effect that benefits everyone in the community.

ppp

"To dare greatly is to dance with destiny, to flirt with failure, and to embrace the unknown with open arms."

ᗞᗞᗞ

SEVENTEEN

THE IMPORTANCE OF FORGIVENESS: TEACHING CHILDREN TO LET GO OF GRUDGES

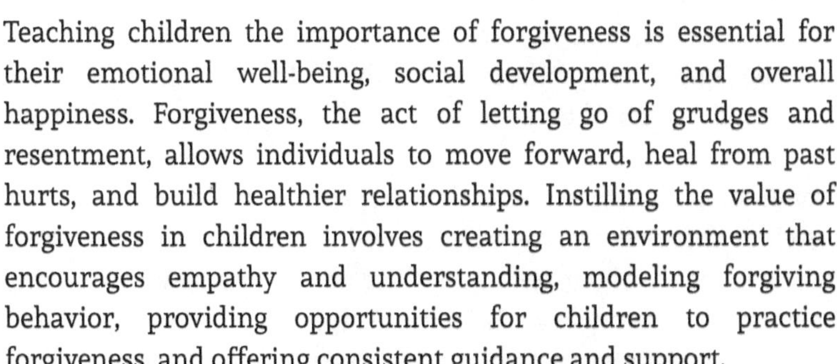

Teaching children the importance of forgiveness is essential for their emotional well-being, social development, and overall happiness. Forgiveness, the act of letting go of grudges and resentment, allows individuals to move forward, heal from past hurts, and build healthier relationships. Instilling the value of forgiveness in children involves creating an environment that encourages empathy and understanding, modeling forgiving behavior, providing opportunities for children to practice forgiveness, and offering consistent guidance and support.

Children begin to encounter situations that require forgiveness from a very young age. Whether it's a sibling taking their toy, a friend saying something hurtful, or a classmate not sharing, these experiences shape their ability to let go of grudges and resolve conflicts. Parents and caregivers play a crucial role in helping children develop forgiveness by creating an environment that supports empathy and understanding, providing consistent reinforcement, and modeling forgiving behavior. When children see adults consistently demonstrating forgiveness in their interactions, they are more likely to adopt these behaviors themselves. This includes everyday actions such as apologizing, making amends, and letting go of past grievances. By showing children what forgiveness looks like, adults can help them develop a clear understanding of the importance of letting go of grudges and moving forward.

Creating an environment that supports forgiveness is essential for fostering this value in children. This involves setting clear expectations for behavior, providing consistent discipline, and creating opportunities for children to practice forgiveness. When children know that forgiveness is expected and valued, they are more likely to develop the skills needed to let go of grudges and resolve conflicts. Positive reinforcement, such as praising and acknowledging forgiving behavior, helps reinforce the importance of forgiveness and encourages children to continue practicing it. For example, saying, "I appreciate how you forgave your friend for their mistake," provides specific feedback that helps children understand the significance of their actions.

Encouraging children to develop empathy is a key component of teaching forgiveness. Empathy, the ability to understand and share the feelings of others, enhances their ability to forgive by helping them see situations from different perspectives. Teaching children to consider the experiences and feelings of others, recognize their own emotions, and understand the impact of their actions helps them develop a greater sense of empathy and a willingness to forgive. Activities such as reading stories about diverse characters, discussing real-life scenarios, and engaging in role-playing exercises can help children develop empathy and a deeper understanding of the importance of forgiveness.

Positive reinforcement is a powerful tool for encouraging forgiveness. When children receive praise and recognition for their forgiving behavior, they are more likely to continue exhibiting these behaviors. Providing specific feedback about what the child did well, such as saying, "I admire how you forgave your classmate and moved on," helps them understand the significance of their actions and reinforces the positive behavior. Additionally, recognizing and celebrating forgiving behavior within the family and community helps create a culture where forgiveness is valued and encouraged.

Teaching children to manage their emotions is essential for helping them develop forgiveness. Forgiveness requires the ability to process and let go of negative emotions, such as anger and resentment. Helping children understand and manage their emotions involves teaching them coping strategies, such as deep breathing, positive self-talk, and mindfulness techniques. Encouraging children to talk about their feelings and providing reassurance and support helps them feel understood and supported. By teaching children to manage their emotions, parents and caregivers can help them develop the resilience and emotional intelligence needed to practice forgiveness.

Providing opportunities for children to practice forgiveness is crucial for reinforcing this value. This can be done through both structured activities and everyday interactions. Encouraging children to apologize and make amends when they have wronged someone, as well as to accept apologies and let go of grievances, helps them develop the skills needed to forgive. Additionally, involving children in family routines that encourage forgiveness, such as resolving conflicts through open communication, expressing feelings constructively, and focusing on solutions rather than blame, helps them understand the importance of forgiveness in daily life.

Helping children develop a growth mindset is also important for fostering forgiveness. A growth mindset is the belief that abilities and intelligence can be developed through effort and perseverance. Encouraging children to view mistakes and conflicts as opportunities for growth, rather than as threats, helps them develop the resilience and positive outlook needed to practice forgiveness. This involves teaching children to embrace challenges, learn from their mistakes, and persist in the face of setbacks. By fostering a growth mindset, parents and caregivers can help children develop the confidence and willingness to forgive, recognizing that everyone makes mistakes and has the capacity for growth and change.

Creating a sense of community and connectedness is essential for nurturing forgiveness. When children feel connected to their family, friends, and community, they are more likely to exhibit forgiving behavior. Encouraging children to build strong, positive relationships with others, participate in community activities, and develop a sense of belonging helps create a supportive environment where forgiveness can flourish. Additionally, teaching children about their responsibilities to others and the importance of contributing to the well-being of their community helps them develop a broader understanding of forgiveness and the impact of their actions on the world around them.

Encouraging children to be kind to themselves is also important for their overall well-being and ability to practice forgiveness. Self-compassion involves recognizing one's own worth, treating oneself with kindness and understanding, and taking care of one's physical and emotional needs. When children learn to be kind to themselves, they develop a positive self-image and a greater capacity for resilience and forgiveness. Encouraging children to practice self-care, recognize their strengths, and treat themselves with kindness helps foster a healthy sense of self-compassion.

Forgiveness is a lifelong value that continues to grow and evolve as children develop. Providing ongoing support, guidance, and reinforcement is essential for helping children navigate the complexities of forgiveness and maintain their commitment to letting go of grudges. Engaging in regular conversations about forgiveness, reflecting on personal experiences, and providing opportunities for children to practice and reinforce forgiving behavior are all important aspects of this process.

Ultimately, teaching children the importance of forgiveness is about helping them recognize the value of letting go of grudges and moving forward with empathy and understanding. By modeling forgiving behavior, creating a supportive environment, and providing consistent reinforcement, parents and caregivers can help children develop the skills and attitudes they need to lead lives based on forgiveness and compassion. Through consistent practice and reinforcement, children can learn to embody forgiveness in their daily interactions and carry this important value into adulthood, contributing to a more harmonious and understanding society. The act of forgiveness not only benefits those who are forgiven but also profoundly impacts those who forgive, allowing them to release negative emotions and build stronger, healthier relationships.

ᗡᗡᗡ

"Within the depths of despair lies the spark of resilience, igniting the flames of hope amidst the darkness."

❥❥❥

EIGHTEEN

Developing Cooperation: Promoting Teamwork and Collaboration

In the journey of raising good humans, one of the paramount attributes to nurture is cooperation. Cooperation is the cornerstone of harmonious relationships, effective teamwork, and collective progress. It involves individuals coming together, pooling their strengths, and working towards common goals. By fostering cooperation in children from a young age, parents, educators, and mentors lay the foundation for their ability to thrive in diverse social settings and contribute positively to society.

At its core, cooperation requires the cultivation of essential social and emotional skills. These include empathy, communication, conflict resolution, and the ability to compromise. Empathy, the capacity to understand and share the feelings of others, serves as the bedrock of cooperation. When children learn to empathize with their peers, they are more inclined to consider their perspectives, collaborate effectively, and forge meaningful connections.

Effective communication is another vital component of cooperation. Clear and respectful communication facilitates the exchange of ideas, ensures mutual understanding, and prevents misunderstandings that may impede collaboration. By teaching children active listening, expressing themselves articulately, and valuing diverse viewpoints, caregivers empower them to engage in constructive dialogue and navigate interpersonal dynamics with ease.

Conflict resolution skills are indispensable in fostering cooperation. Conflicts are inevitable in any social setting, but how they are resolved determines the quality of relationships and the cohesion of groups. Children who are adept at resolving conflicts peacefully, negotiating compromises, and seeking win-win solutions are better equipped to navigate interpersonal challenges and sustain harmonious interactions.

Moreover, cooperation entails the capacity to compromise. In collaborative endeavors, individuals may have differing perspectives or preferences. The ability to find common ground, make concessions, and prioritize collective interests over personal desires fosters cohesion and propels the group towards shared objectives. By instilling the value of compromise in children, caregivers equip them with a crucial life skill that underpins successful relationships and collaborative endeavors.

In cultivating cooperation, it is essential to create conducive environments that encourage and reinforce collaborative behaviors. Families, classrooms, and communities serve as the primary contexts within which children learn and practice cooperation. By modeling cooperative behaviors, providing opportunities for collaboration, and offering positive reinforcement, caregivers facilitate the development of cooperation in children.

Modeling cooperative behaviors entails demonstrating empathy, effective communication, conflict resolution, and compromise in everyday interactions. Children observe and internalize the behaviors modeled by adults, making it imperative for caregivers to embody the values they seek to instill. By consistently modeling cooperation in their interactions with others, caregivers serve as powerful role models and shape children's attitudes and behaviors towards collaboration.

Providing opportunities for collaboration is equally crucial in nurturing cooperation. Activities that require teamwork, such as group projects, cooperative games, and community service initiatives, offer valuable learning experiences where children can practice cooperation in real-world contexts. These experiences not only enhance children's social and emotional skills but also foster a sense of belonging and interconnectedness within the group.

Furthermore, offering positive reinforcement reinforces cooperative behaviors and motivates children to continue exhibiting them. Praise, encouragement, and recognition for acts of cooperation reinforce the value of collaborative efforts and cultivate a positive culture of cooperation within families, classrooms, and communities. By celebrating and acknowledging children's contributions to collective endeavors, caregivers reinforce the importance of cooperation and inspire them to engage in future collaborations enthusiastically.

In addition to creating conducive environments, caregivers can employ various strategies to promote cooperation in children effectively. Encouraging perspective-taking, fostering a sense of belonging, and teaching problem-solving skills are among the strategies that facilitate the development of cooperation in children.

Encouraging perspective-taking involves helping children understand and appreciate different viewpoints. By exposing children to diverse perspectives, encouraging them to consider others' thoughts and feelings, and discussing the impact of their actions on others, caregivers foster empathy and enhance children's ability to cooperate effectively. Perspective-taking enables children to recognize the value of diversity, respect individual differences, and collaborate inclusively with others.

Fostering a sense of belonging is essential in cultivating cooperation. When children feel valued, accepted, and connected to their family, school, or community, they are more motivated to contribute positively and cooperate with others. Caregivers can nurture a sense of belonging by creating inclusive environments, fostering positive relationships, and providing opportunities for children to actively participate and contribute to the group.

Moreover, teaching problem-solving skills equips children with the tools to navigate challenges and conflicts constructively. By teaching children strategies for identifying problems, generating alternative solutions, evaluating their effectiveness, and implementing solutions collaboratively, caregivers empower them to address issues that arise in social interactions effectively. Problem-solving skills enable children to resolve conflicts, overcome obstacles, and achieve shared goals through cooperation and collaboration.

Cooperation is a fundamental skill that underpins harmonious relationships, effective teamwork, and collective progress. By fostering cooperation in children through the cultivation of essential social and emotional skills, creating conducive environments, and employing effective strategies, caregivers play a pivotal role in shaping children's ability to thrive in diverse social settings and contribute positively to society. As children learn to cooperate, they develop the empathy, communication, conflict resolution, and compromise skills needed to navigate the complexities of human interaction and build a more compassionate and interconnected world.

❦❦❦

"To bloom amidst adversity is the truest testament to the indomitable spirit of the human soul."

NINETEEN

THE POWER OF CURIOSITY: ENCOURAGING A LOVE FOR LEARNING

Encouraging a love for learning in children is a powerful and transformative endeavor. Curiosity, the innate desire to explore and understand the world, drives the quest for knowledge and fuels intellectual development. Fostering curiosity involves creating an environment that stimulates inquisitiveness, modeling curious behavior, providing opportunities for exploration, and offering consistent support and encouragement. By nurturing curiosity, parents and caregivers can help children develop a lifelong passion for learning, enhance their problem-solving skills, and promote creativity and innovation.

Children are naturally curious from a very young age, often asking endless questions about their surroundings. This innate curiosity is a critical aspect of their cognitive development, helping them make sense of the world and build a foundation for future learning. Parents and caregivers play a crucial role in maintaining and enhancing this curiosity by creating an environment that encourages exploration and discovery. This involves providing a variety of stimulating materials and experiences, such as books, toys, nature walks, and science experiments, that captivate children's interests and inspire them to learn more.

Modeling curious behavior is one of the most effective ways to teach children the value of curiosity. When children see adults engaging in activities that demonstrate a love for learning, they are more likely to adopt these behaviors themselves. This includes asking questions, seeking out new experiences, and expressing enthusiasm for discovering new information. By showing children that curiosity is a lifelong pursuit, adults can help them understand the importance of remaining inquisitive and open to new ideas throughout their lives.

Creating opportunities for children to explore their interests is essential for fostering curiosity. This can be done through both structured activities and unstructured play. Encouraging children to pursue their interests, whether it's through reading books, conducting experiments, building models, or engaging in imaginative play, helps them develop a sense of agency and ownership over their learning. Providing a wide range of experiences and exposing children to different fields of knowledge can also help them discover new passions and expand their horizons.

Positive reinforcement is a powerful tool for encouraging curiosity. When children receive praise and recognition for their inquisitive behavior, they are more likely to continue exploring and asking questions. Providing specific feedback about what the child did well, such as saying, "I admire how you asked questions to learn more about the topic," helps them understand the significance of their actions and reinforces the positive behavior. Additionally, recognizing and celebrating curious behavior within the family and community helps create a culture where a love for learning is valued and encouraged.

Teaching children to embrace challenges and view them as opportunities for growth is also crucial for fostering curiosity. A growth mindset, the belief that abilities and intelligence can be developed through effort and perseverance, helps children approach new experiences with enthusiasm and a willingness to learn. Encouraging children to take risks, make mistakes, and learn from their experiences promotes resilience and a positive outlook toward learning. By fostering a growth mindset, parents and caregivers can help children develop the confidence and curiosity needed to explore new ideas and overcome obstacles.

Providing opportunities for children to engage in hands-on learning experiences is essential for nurturing curiosity. Experiential learning, where children actively participate in the learning process through experimentation, observation, and problem-solving, helps them develop a deeper understanding of concepts and retain information more effectively. Activities such as science experiments, nature exploration, art projects, and building challenges provide children with the opportunity to ask questions, test hypotheses, and discover answers through direct interaction with their environment.

Encouraging children to ask questions and seek answers is a key component of developing curiosity. Creating an open and supportive environment where children feel comfortable expressing their curiosity helps them develop critical thinking skills and a love for learning. Responding to children's questions with interest and enthusiasm, and providing opportunities for them to find answers through research, experimentation, and exploration, reinforces the value of curiosity and promotes intellectual growth.

Helping children develop strong research and inquiry skills is also important for fostering curiosity. Teaching children how to find reliable sources of information, evaluate the credibility of different sources, and synthesize information from various perspectives helps them become independent learners and critical thinkers. Encouraging children to explore different methods of inquiry, such as reading, conducting experiments, and interviewing experts, provides them with the tools they need to satisfy their curiosity and deepen their understanding of the world.

Creating a sense of community and connectedness is essential for nurturing curiosity. When children feel supported and connected to their family, friends, and community, they are more likely to engage in curious behavior. Encouraging children to build strong, positive relationships with others, participate in group activities, and share their discoveries and questions with others helps create a supportive environment where curiosity can flourish. Additionally, teaching children about their responsibilities to others and the importance of contributing to the well-being of their community helps them develop a broader understanding of curiosity and the impact of their actions on the world around them.

Encouraging children to be kind to themselves is also important for their overall well-being and ability to practice curiosity. Self-compassion involves recognizing one's own worth, treating oneself with kindness and understanding, and taking care of one's physical and emotional needs. When children learn to be kind to themselves, they develop a positive self-image and a greater capacity for resilience and curiosity. Encouraging children to practice self-care, recognize their strengths, and treat themselves with kindness helps foster a healthy sense of self-compassion.

Curiosity is a lifelong value that continues to grow and evolve as children develop. Providing ongoing support, guidance, and reinforcement is essential for helping children navigate the complexities of curiosity and maintain their commitment to a love for learning. Engaging in regular conversations about curiosity, reflecting on personal experiences, and providing opportunities for children to practice and reinforce inquisitive behavior are all important aspects of this process.

Ultimately, encouraging curiosity in children is about helping them recognize the importance of maintaining a love for learning throughout their lives. By modeling curious behavior, creating a supportive environment, and providing consistent reinforcement, parents and caregivers can help children develop the skills and attitudes they need to lead lives based on curiosity and intellectual growth. Through consistent practice and reinforcement, children can learn to embody curiosity in their daily interactions and carry this important value into adulthood, contributing to a more innovative and knowledge-driven society. The power of curiosity not only enriches the lives of those who embrace it but also drives progress and discovery in all areas of human endeavor.

"In the mosaic of life, every shattered piece finds its place, creating a masterpiece of resilience and redemption."

ᗪᗪᗪ

TWENTY

Fostering Peacefulness: Teaching Conflict Resolution and Calmness

Fostering peacefulness in children is fundamental to their emotional well-being and social development. Teaching conflict resolution and calmness equips children with the skills they need to navigate the complexities of human interactions and manage their emotions effectively. By creating an environment that promotes peacefulness, modeling calm behavior, providing opportunities for children to practice conflict resolution, and offering consistent guidance and support, parents and caregivers can help children develop the ability to resolve disputes amicably and maintain a sense of inner peace.

From an early age, children experience conflicts in various forms, whether with siblings, peers, or even adults. These conflicts provide valuable learning opportunities to develop skills for managing disagreements and maintaining harmonious relationships. Parents and caregivers play a crucial role in guiding children through these experiences by setting clear expectations, providing consistent discipline, and modeling peaceful behavior. When children see adults handling conflicts calmly and constructively, they are more likely to adopt these behaviors themselves. This includes actions such as listening actively, expressing feelings respectfully, and seeking mutually beneficial solutions. By demonstrating what peaceful conflict resolution looks like, adults can help children understand the importance of resolving disputes without resorting to aggression or hostility.

Creating an environment that supports peacefulness is essential for fostering this value in children. This involves setting clear expectations for behavior, providing consistent discipline, and creating opportunities for children to practice calmness and conflict resolution. When children know that peacefulness is expected and valued, they are more likely to develop the skills needed to manage conflicts and maintain a sense of calm. Positive reinforcement, such as praising and acknowledging calm and peaceful behavior, helps reinforce the importance of these qualities and encourages children to continue practicing them. For example, saying, "I appreciate how you stayed calm and worked through the disagreement with your friend," provides specific feedback that helps children understand the significance of their actions.

Encouraging children to develop empathy is a key component of teaching peacefulness. Empathy, the ability to understand and share the feelings of others, enhances their ability to resolve conflicts amicably. Teaching children to consider the experiences and emotions of others, recognize their own feelings, and understand the impact of their actions helps them develop a greater sense of empathy and a willingness to resolve conflicts peacefully. Activities such as reading stories about diverse characters, discussing real-life scenarios, and engaging in role-playing exercises can help children develop empathy and a deeper understanding of the importance of peaceful conflict resolution.

Teaching children to manage their emotions is essential for helping them develop peacefulness. Calmness requires the ability to stay composed and collected in the face of stress and frustration. Helping children understand and manage their emotions involves teaching them coping strategies, such as deep breathing, positive self-talk, and mindfulness techniques. Encouraging children to talk about their feelings and providing reassurance and support helps them feel understood and supported. By teaching children to manage their emotions, parents and caregivers can help them develop the resilience and self-control needed to practice peacefulness.

Providing opportunities for children to practice conflict resolution is crucial for reinforcing this value. This can be done through both structured activities and everyday interactions. Encouraging children to express their feelings constructively, listen to others, and seek mutually agreeable solutions helps them develop the skills needed to resolve conflicts peacefully. Additionally, involving children in family routines that encourage calmness and conflict resolution, such as discussing problems openly, expressing feelings respectfully, and focusing on solutions rather than blame, helps them understand the importance of these practices in daily life.

Helping children develop problem-solving skills is also important for fostering peacefulness. When children learn to identify problems, think critically about solutions, and take action to resolve issues, they develop a sense of confidence and competence. Encouraging children to brainstorm solutions to challenges, make decisions, and evaluate the outcomes of their actions helps them build the skills they need to manage conflicts and make responsible choices. This includes teaching children to learn from their mistakes and view challenges as opportunities for growth and learning.

Creating a sense of community and connectedness is essential for nurturing peacefulness. When children feel connected to their family, friends, and community, they are more likely to exhibit calm and peaceful behavior. Encouraging children to build strong, positive relationships with others, participate in community activities, and develop a sense of belonging helps create a supportive environment where peacefulness can flourish. Additionally, teaching children about their responsibilities to others and the importance of contributing to the well-being of their community helps them develop a broader understanding of peacefulness and the impact of their actions on the world around them.

Encouraging children to be kind to themselves is also important for their overall well-being and ability to practice peacefulness. Self-compassion involves recognizing one's own worth, treating oneself with kindness and understanding, and taking care of one's physical and emotional needs. When children learn to be kind to themselves, they develop a positive self-image and a greater capacity for resilience and calmness. Encouraging children to practice self-care, recognize their strengths, and treat themselves with kindness helps foster a healthy sense of self-compassion.

Peacefulness is a lifelong value that continues to grow and evolve as children develop. Providing ongoing support, guidance, and reinforcement is essential for helping children navigate the complexities of peacefulness and maintain their commitment to calmness and conflict resolution. Engaging in regular conversations about peacefulness, reflecting on personal experiences, and providing opportunities for children to practice and reinforce calm and peaceful behavior are all important aspects of this process.

Ultimately, fostering peacefulness in children is about helping them recognize the importance of resolving conflicts amicably and maintaining a sense of inner calm. By modeling peaceful behavior, creating a supportive environment, and providing consistent reinforcement, parents and caregivers can help children develop the skills and attitudes they need to lead lives based on peacefulness and empathy. Through consistent practice and reinforcement, children can learn to embody peacefulness in their daily interactions and carry this important value into adulthood, contributing to a more harmonious and understanding society. The ability to resolve conflicts peacefully and maintain calmness not only benefits those who practice it but also creates a ripple effect that promotes peace and cooperation in the broader community.

"Like a phoenix, rise from the ashes of despair, for it
is in the darkest moments that the brightest stars
are born."

♡♡♡

TWENTY-ONE
SUMMARY

Raising children with strong moral character and social responsibility is a multifaceted endeavor that involves instilling a variety of values and skills. Each of these values, from kindness and honesty to perseverance and curiosity, contributes to the overall development of a child's character and ability to interact positively with the world. The goal is to help children grow into compassionate, resilient, and responsible adults who can navigate life's challenges with integrity and empathy.

One of the most fundamental aspects of character development is teaching children about the foundation of character, which includes understanding the basics of moral development. This process begins early, as children observe and learn from the behaviors, attitudes, and values of those around them.

A secure and nurturing environment is crucial, as it provides a safe space for children to explore and learn about empathy, respect, honesty, kindness, responsibility, courage, patience, and gratitude. Parents and caregivers play a pivotal role by modeling these behaviors and reinforcing their importance through consistent guidance and support.

Empathy is a key component of moral development, enabling

children to connect with others on an emotional level. Teaching empathy involves modeling empathetic behavior, encouraging children to express their feelings, and helping them consider the perspectives of others. Activities such as reading stories and engaging in role-playing can enhance a child's ability to empathize with others.

Respect is another foundational element that involves recognizing the inherent worth of oneself and others. Teaching respect includes setting clear expectations for behavior, modeling respectful interactions, and providing consistent discipline. When children learn to respect themselves and those around them, they build healthy relationships and contribute to a harmonious society.

Honesty is essential for building trust and credibility. Fostering honesty in children involves creating an environment where they feel safe to tell the truth, encouraging open communication, and addressing dishonesty constructively. Children should understand that honesty is not only about telling the truth but also about living authentically and with integrity.

Kindness enhances the quality of life for both the giver and the receiver. Teaching kindness involves encouraging children to think about how their actions affect others and to engage in acts of generosity and compassion. Recognizing and celebrating kind behaviors reinforces the importance of kindness in daily life.

Responsibility involves taking ownership of one's actions and understanding their impact on oneself and others. Teaching responsibility requires giving children age-appropriate tasks and allowing them to experience the consequences of their actions. By holding children accountable and helping them learn from their mistakes, parents and caregivers prepare them to be responsible and conscientious individuals.

Courage is the ability to face challenges and adversity with strength and determination. Teaching courage involves creating a supportive environment where children feel encouraged to take risks and try new things. Celebrating efforts rather than just successes helps build resilience and bravery.

Patience is the ability to wait calmly and without frustration. Teaching patience involves modeling calm behavior, setting realistic expectations, and providing opportunities for children to practice waiting. Engaging in activities that require delayed gratification can help children develop patience and understand the value of persistence.

Gratitude is the practice of recognizing and appreciating the positive aspects of life. Teaching gratitude involves encouraging children to express thanks for the people, experiences, and things they value. Practices such as keeping a gratitude journal and writing thank-you notes can help instill gratitude as a daily habit.

Humility involves recognizing one's limitations and valuing the contributions of others. Teaching humility requires modeling modest behavior, encouraging children to acknowledge their mistakes, and helping them understand that everyone has unique strengths and weaknesses.

Balancing self-esteem with humility ensures that children feel confident and capable while being respectful and appreciative of others.

Generosity involves the willingness to give and share without expecting anything in return. Teaching generosity involves encouraging children to share their time, resources, and talents with others. Participating in charitable activities and discussing the importance of helping others can help foster a generous spirit.

Self-discipline is the ability to control one's impulses and behaviors. Teaching self-discipline requires setting clear expectations, providing consistent consequences, and encouraging children to practice self-control. Activities that require focus and perseverance can help children develop self-discipline.

Perseverance is the ability to keep going despite difficulties and setbacks. Teaching perseverance involves encouraging children to set goals, providing support and encouragement, and helping them learn from their mistakes. Celebrating efforts and progress helps build resilience and determination.

Optimism is the practice of focusing on the positive aspects of life and maintaining a hopeful outlook. Teaching optimism involves modeling positive behavior, encouraging children to reframe negative situations, and helping them focus on their strengths and successes. Engaging in activities that promote positive thinking can help nurture an optimistic mindset.

Service is the act of helping others and contributing to the community. Teaching service involves providing opportunities for children to engage in acts of kindness and volunteerism. Discussing the impact of their actions and encouraging them to think about how they can make a difference helps instill a sense of responsibility and generosity.

Fairness involves treating others equitably and justly. Teaching fairness requires modeling fair behavior, setting clear rules and expectations, and encouraging children to consider the perspectives of others. Engaging in discussions about fairness and providing opportunities to practice fair decision-making helps foster a sense of equality and integrity.

Forgiveness is the ability to let go of resentment and move forward after being wronged. Teaching forgiveness involves modeling forgiving behavior, encouraging children to express their feelings, and helping them understand the importance of letting go of grudges.

Discussing the benefits of forgiveness and providing opportunities to practice it helps nurture a forgiving and compassionate spirit.

Cooperation involves working together towards a common goal. Teaching cooperation requires providing opportunities for children to engage in group activities, encouraging teamwork, and modeling cooperative behavior. Discussing the importance of collaboration and helping children understand the value of different perspectives helps foster a sense of unity and mutual respect.

Curiosity is the desire to learn and explore. Teaching curiosity involves encouraging children to ask questions, providing opportunities for exploration and discovery, and modeling a curious mindset. Engaging in activities that stimulate curiosity helps nurture a sense of wonder and intellectual growth.

Peacefulness involves maintaining calm and resolving conflicts harmoniously. Teaching peacefulness involves modeling calm behavior, providing opportunities to practice relaxation techniques, and encouraging children to resolve conflicts respectfully. Engaging in activities that promote mindfulness and emotional regulation helps nurture a sense of peace and tranquility.

By nurturing these values and skills, parents and caregivers can help children develop into well-rounded, compassionate, and responsible individuals. Each value contributes to the overall development of a child's character and ability to interact positively with the world.

Through consistent modeling, positive reinforcement, and creating an environment that fosters growth and learning, children can internalize these values and carry them into adulthood.

This holistic approach to character development not only benefits the individual child but also contributes to the creation of a more compassionate, resilient, and responsible society. By investing in the moral and ethical development of children, we are laying the foundation for a better future for all.

❧❧❧

Citation And References

This book represents the culmination of extensive research and meticulous analysis, incorporating a diverse range of sources, including numerous books, scholarly studies, and personal experiences. Additionally, I have scoured various websites to gather relevant information and data essential for the compilation of this work. I have taken every precaution to ensure the accuracy of the information presented and have diligently cited all sources to acknowledge their contributions.

Despite these efforts, the possibility of inadvertent errors remains. I deeply value the insights of my readers and appreciate any feedback that can help identify and rectify such inaccuracies. I encourage you to bring any discrepancies to my attention.

Your feedback is not only welcome but crucial, as it will aid in correcting current editions and enhancing the content of future ones. I am committed to maintaining the highest standards of accuracy and reliability in my work and thank you for your support and understanding.

Additionally, I firmly uphold the principle of freedom of speech and expression as guaranteed under Article 19(1)(a) of the Constitution of India, and I respect the diverse viewpoints and expressions of all readers.

ᐚᐚᐚ

Other Books Of The Author

1. Empowering Minds: A Journey into Women's Self-Discovery and Power
2. The Dynamics of Motivation: Catalyzing Thought into Action
3. Meditation and Mental Well Being: The Path to Inner Peace and Clarity
4. The Psychology of Child Education: Nurturing Future Generations
5. Ethical Enlightenment: A Modern Guide to Living with Integrity
6. Voices of Empowerment: Stories of Women Rising Against Odds
7. Social Psychology in Everyday Life: Understanding Human Connections
8. The Essence of Motivational Speaking: Inspiring Change in Others
9. Balancing Acts: Women, Work, and the Will to Lead
10. Guiding with Grace: Raising Children with Compassion and Awareness
11. The Power of Positive Aging: Embracing Life After Fifty
12. Building Resilient Communities: Social Work in Action
13. The Ethical Educator: Principles for Teaching and Learning
14. From Insight to Impact: Social Psychology for a Better World
15. The Ethics of Empathy: A Guide to Ethical Living
16. The Science of Empowering the Self: Navigating Life's Challenges with Psychological Wisdom
17. The Mindful Conscious Leader: Meditation Techniques for Modern Management
18. Pioneering Spirit: Women's Pathways to Leadership and Empowerment
19. Feeling to Healing: The Role of Emotional Intelligence in Child Development
20. Transformative Talks and Words of Inspiration: Insights into Motivational Oratory

Bhajan
101. Pilgrimage of the Soul: Spiritual Journeys in India

ಬಿಬಿಬಿ

Contact

Dr. Minakshi Bansal
Social Activist
Ahmedabad, Gujarat, Bharat
minakshiindiag20@yahoo.com

❦❦❦

|| LOKAHA SAMASTHAHA SUKHINO BHAVANTU ||